WESTERN WORLD
GEOGRAPHY

Guided Reading Workbook

Contents

Guided Reading Workbook

How to Use This Book

The *Guided Reading Workbook* was developed to help you get the most from your reading. Using this workbook alongside your textbook will help you master geography content while developing your reading and vocabulary skills. Reviewing the next few pages before getting started will make you aware of the many useful features in this book.

Lesson summary pages allow you to interact with the content and key terms and places from each section of a module. The summaries explain each section of your textbook in a way that is easy to understand.

Lesson numbers make it easy to find your place in the workbook.

The main idea statements help focus your attention as you read the summaries.

Definitions for the key terms and places from your textbook are given.

Headings under each lesson summary match those of your textbook, which can help you find the material you need.

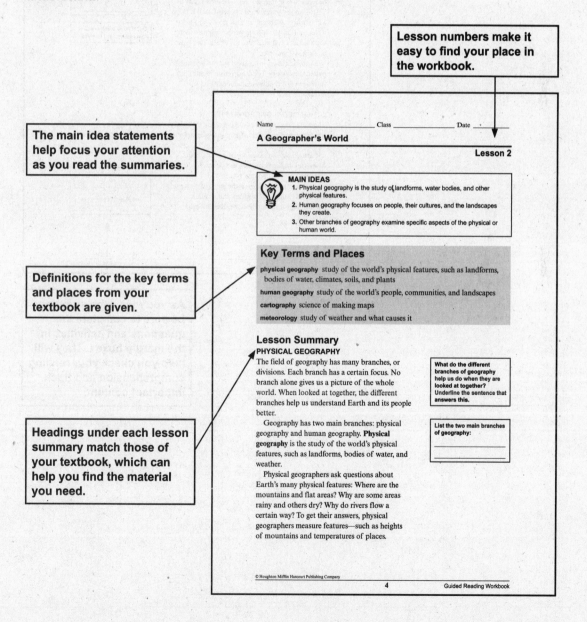

Name _____ Class _____ Date _____
A Geographer's World

Lesson 2

MAIN IDEAS
1. Physical geography is the study of landforms, water bodies, and other physical features.
2. Human geography focuses on people, their cultures, and the landscapes they create.
3. Other branches of geography examine specific aspects of the physical or human world.

Key Terms and Places

physical geography study of the world's physical features, such as landforms, bodies of water, climates, soils, and plants

human geography study of the world's people, communities, and landscapes

cartography science of making maps

meteorology study of weather and what causes it

Lesson Summary
PHYSICAL GEOGRAPHY
The field of geography has many branches, or divisions. Each branch has a certain focus. No branch alone gives us a picture of the whole world. When looked at together, the different branches help us understand Earth and its people better.

Geography has two main branches: physical geography and human geography. **Physical geography** is the study of the world's physical features, such as landforms, bodies of water, and weather.

Physical geographers ask questions about Earth's many physical features: Where are the mountains and flat areas? Why are some areas rainy and others dry? Why do rivers flow a certain way? To get their answers, physical geographers measure features—such as heights of mountains and temperatures of places.

What do the different branches of geography help us do when they are looked at together? Underline the sentence that answers this.

List the two main branches of geography:
_____
_____

© Houghton Mifflin Harcourt Publishing Company

4   Guided Reading Workbook

The key terms and places from your textbook have been boldfaced, allowing you to quickly find and study them.

Name _____ Class _____ Date _____

Lesson 2, *continued*

Physical geography has important uses. It helps us understand how the world works. It also helps us predict and prepare for dangerous storms.

HUMAN GEOGRAPHY

Human geography is the other main branch of geography. It is the study of people and their communities and landscapes.

Human geographers study people in the past or present. They ask questions such as why people choose to live in certain places. They might investigate what kinds of work people do.

People all over the world are very different, so human geographers often study a smaller topic. They might study people in one region, such as central Africa. They might study one part of people's lives in different regions, such as city life.

Human geography has important uses. It helps us learn how people meet basic needs for food, water, and shelter. It helps people improve their communities and measures the effects they have on the environment.

Historians use human geography to investigate patterns in history. These help them identify turning points that brought about historic changes to society.

OTHER FIELDS OF GEOGRAPHY

There are other branches of geography that study smaller specialized parts of physical geography or human geography.

Cartography is the science of making maps. Maps can display locations, as well as information about people, places, and environments. Hydrology is the study of water on Earth, including river systems and rainfall. **Meteorology** is the study of weather and what causes it.

> Why do human geographers often study one smaller topic?
> _____
> _____
> _____

> Circle three basic needs that people have to meet.

> What is meteorology?
> _____
> _____
> _____

© Houghton Mifflin Harcourt Publishing Company

5   Guided Reading Workbook

As you read each summary, be sure to complete the questions and activities in the margin boxes. They will help you check your reading comprehension and track important content.

Each lesson has activities that allow you to demonstrate your understanding of the lesson's key terms and places. Use the lesson summaries and your textbook to answer these activities.

The challenge activity provides an opportunity for you to apply important critical thinking skills using the content that you learned in the lesson.

A variety of activities helps you check your knowledge of key terms and places.

Some pages have a word bank. You can use it to help find answers or complete writing activities.

Writing activities require you to include key words and places in what you write. Remember to check to make sure you are using the terms and places correctly.

Name _____ Class _____ Date _____

Lesson 2, *continued*

CHALLENGE ACTIVITY

Critical Thinking: Draw Inferences Examine a map of an unfamiliar city using a road atlas or an online map. Write a paragraph telling a visitor what physical and human features to look for in each quadrant (NE, SE, NW, SW).

DIRECTIONS Read each sentence, and fill in the blank with the word in the word pair that best completes the sentence.

1. _____ is the study of weather and what causes it. (**Cartography/Meteorology**)

2. Geographers might study _____ if they want to know how Victoria Falls was formed. (**physical geography/human geography**)

3. Without _____, geographers would not be able to use maps to study where things are in the world. (**cartography/meteorology**)

4. The study of Earth's people, including their ways of life, homes, cities, beliefs, and customs, is called _____. (**physical geography/human geography**)

5. Studying the world's river systems and how to protect the world's water supply are important parts of _____. (**hydrology/meteorology**)

cartography	human geography	hydrology
meteorology	physical geography	

DIRECTIONS Look up the vocabulary terms in the word bank in a dictionary. Write the dictionary definition of the word that is closest to the definition used in your textbook.

_____

_____

_____

_____

_____

6   Guided Reading Workbook

A Geographer's World

MAIN IDEAS
1. Geography is the study of the world, its people, and the landscapes they create.
2. Geographers look at the world in many different ways.

Key Terms and Places

geography study of the world, its people, and the landscapes they create

landscape human and physical features that make a place unique

social science field that studies people and the relationships among them

region part of the world with one or more common features distinguishing it from surrounding areas

Lesson Summary
WHAT IS GEOGRAPHY?

For every place on Earth, you can ask questions to learn about it: What does the land look like? What is the weather like? What are people's lives like? Asking questions like these is how you study geography. **Geography** is the study of the world, its people, and the physical and human **landscapes** that make a place unique.

Geographers (people who study geography) ask questions about how the world works. For example, they may ask why a place gets tornadoes. To find answers, they gather data by observing and measuring. Then they study and interpret the data. In this way, geography is like science.

Geography can also be like a social science. **Social science** studies people and how they relate to each other. This information cannot be measured in the same way. To study people, geographers may visit places and talk to the people about their lives.

Underline the sentences that state how geography is like science.

LOOKING AT THE WORLD

Geographers must look carefully at the world around them. Depending on what they want to learn, they look at the world at different levels.

Geographers may study at the local level, such as a city or town. They may ask why people live there, what work they do, and how they travel. They can help a town or city plan improvements.

Geographers may also study at the regional level. A **region** is an area with common features. A region may be big or small. Its features make it different from areas around it. The features may be physical (such as mountains) or human (such as language).

Sometimes geographers study at the global level. They study how people interact all over the world. Geographers can help us learn how people's actions affect other people and places. For example, they may ask how one region influences other regions.

> Circle the three levels that geographers study.

CHALLENGE ACTIVITY

Critical Thinking: Evaluate Find a map of your state. Determine the state's different regions based on physical characteristics. Are there regions with mountains, ones near important bodies of water, regions that rely on farming, or areas with lots of cities? Make a list of the regions and each one's characteristics. Which region do you live in?

DIRECTIONS On the line provided before each statement, write **T** if the statement is true and **F** if the statement is false. If the statement is false, write the correct term on the line after each sentence that makes the sentence a true statement.

_____ 1. The study of the world, its people, and the landscapes they create is called <u>geography</u>.

_____

_____ 2. Geography is sometimes called a <u>social science</u> because it studies people and the relationships among them.

_____

_____ 3. An example of a small <u>region</u> that geographers might study is Chinatown in San Francisco.

_____

_____ 4. The combination of human and physical features that make a place unique is called a <u>landscape</u>.

_____

_____ 5. When geographers study how people live on a <u>global level</u>, they look at a single city or town.

_____

A Geographer's World

MAIN IDEAS
1. Physical geography is the study of landforms, water bodies, and other physical features.
2. Human geography focuses on people, their cultures, and the landscapes they create.
3. Other branches of geography examine specific aspects of the physical or human world.

Key Terms and Places

physical geography study of the world's physical features, such as landforms, bodies of water, climates, soils, and plants

human geography study of the world's people, communities, and landscapes

cartography science of making maps

meteorology study of weather and what causes it

Lesson Summary
PHYSICAL GEOGRAPHY

The field of geography has many branches, or divisions. Each branch has a certain focus. No branch alone gives us a picture of the whole world. When looked at together, the different branches help us understand Earth and its people better.

Geography has two main branches: physical geography and human geography. **Physical geography** is the study of the world's physical features, such as landforms, bodies of water, and weather.

Physical geographers ask questions about Earth's many physical features: Where are the mountains and flat areas? Why are some areas rainy and others dry? Why do rivers flow a certain way? To get their answers, physical geographers measure features—such as heights of mountains and temperatures of places.

> What do the different branches of geography help us do when they are looked at together? Underline the sentence that answers this.

> List the two main branches of geography:
> _____
> _____

Physical geography has important uses. It helps us understand how the world works. It also helps us predict and prepare for dangerous storms.

HUMAN GEOGRAPHY

Human geography is the other main branch of geography. It is the study of people and their communities and landscapes.

Human geographers study people in the past or present. They ask questions such as why people choose to live in certain places. They might investigate what kinds of work people do.

People all over the world are very different, so human geographers often study a smaller topic. They might study people in one region, such as central Africa. They might study one part of people's lives in different regions, such as city life.

> **Why do human geographers often study one smaller topic?**
>
> _____
> _____
> _____

Human geography has important uses. It helps us learn how people meet basic needs for food, water, and shelter. It helps people improve their communities and measures the effects they have on the environment.

> **Circle three basic needs that people have to meet.**

Historians use human geography to investigate patterns in history. These help them identify turning points that brought about historic changes to society.

OTHER FIELDS OF GEOGRAPHY

There are other branches of geography that study smaller specialized parts of physical geography or human geography.

Cartography is the science of making maps. Maps can display locations, as well as information about people, places, and environments. Hydrology is the study of water on Earth, including river systems and rainfall. **Meteorology** is the study of weather and what causes it.

> **What is meteorology?**
>
> _____
> _____
> _____

CHALLENGE ACTIVITY

Critical Thinking: Draw Inferences Examine a map of an unfamiliar city using a road atlas or an online map. Write a paragraph telling a visitor what physical and human features to look for in each quadrant (NE, SE, NW, SW).

DIRECTIONS Read each sentence, and fill in the blank with the word in the word pair that best completes the sentence.

1. _____ is the study of weather and what causes it.
   (Cartography/Meteorology)

2. Geographers might study _____ if they want to know how Victoria Falls was formed. **(physical geography/human geography)**

3. Without _____, geographers would not be able to use maps to study where things are in the world. **(cartography/meteorology)**

4. The study of Earth's people, including their ways of life, homes, cities, beliefs, and customs, is called _____. **(physical geography/human geography)**

5. Studying the world's river systems and how to protect the world's water supply are important parts of _____. **(hydrology/meteorology)**

cartography	human geography	hydrology
meteorology	physical geography	

DIRECTIONS Look up the vocabulary terms in the word bank in a dictionary. Write the dictionary definition of the word that is closest to the definition used in your textbook.

_____

_____

_____

_____

_____

A Geographer's World

Lesson 3

> **MAIN IDEAS**
> 1. The five themes of geography help us organize our studies of the world.
> 2. The six essential elements of geography highlight some of the subject's most important ideas.

Key Terms and Places

absolute location specific description of where a place is

relative location general description of where a place is

environment an area's land, water, climate, plants and animals, and other physical features

Lesson Summary
THE FIVE THEMES OF GEOGRAPHY

Geographers use themes in their work. A theme is a topic that is common throughout a discussion or event. Many holidays have a theme, such as the flag and patriotism on the Fourth of July.

There are five major themes of geography: Location, Place, Human-Environment Interaction, Movement, and Regions. Geographers can use these themes in almost everything they study.

Location describes where a place is. This may be specific, such as an address. This is called an **absolute location.** It may also be general, such as saying the United States is north of Central America. This is called a **relative location.**

Place refers to an area's landscape. The landscape is made up of the physical and human features of a place, such as the land, climate, or people. Together, these features give a place its own identity apart from other places.

Human-Environment Interaction studies how people and their environment affect each other. The **environment** includes an area's physical

List the five major themes of geography:
_____
_____
_____
_____

features, such as land, water, weather, and animals. Geographers study how people change their environment (by building dams or towns, for example). They also study how the environment causes people to adapt (by dressing for the weather, for example).

Movement involves learning about why and how people move. Do they move for work or pleasure? Do they travel by roads or other routes?

Studying Regions helps geographers learn how places are alike and different. This also helps them learn why places developed the way they did.

> **Describe two ways that people and their environment affect each other.**
>
> _____
>
> _____
>
> _____
>
> _____

THE SIX ESSENTIAL ELEMENTS

It is important to organize how you study geography so you get the most complete picture of a place. Using the five major themes can help you do this. Using the six essential elements can, too.

Geographers and teachers created the six elements from 18 basic ideas, called standards. The standards say what everyone should understand about geography. Each element groups together the standards that are related to each other.

The six elements are The World in Spatial Terms (*spatial* refers to where places are located), Places and Regions, Physical Systems, Human Systems, Environment and Society, and Uses of Geography. The six elements build on the five themes, so some elements and themes are similar. Uses of Geography is not part of the five themes. It focuses on how people can use geography to learn about the past and present and plan for the future.

> **What do the five themes and six elements of geography help you do? Underline the sentence that explains this.**

CHALLENGE ACTIVITY

Critical Thinking: Analyze Analyze a place you regularly visit, such as a vacation spot or a park in your neighborhood. Write a question about the place for each geography theme to help someone not familiar with the themes to understand them.

DIRECTIONS Write a word or phrase that has the same meaning as
the term given.

1. absolute location _____

_____

2. element _____

_____

3. environment _____

_____

4. interaction _____

_____

5. relative location _____

_____

absolute location	element	environment
interaction	relative location	

DIRECTIONS Choose at least four of the vocabulary words from the
word bank. Use these words to write a story or poem that relates to
the lesson.

_____

_____

_____

_____

_____

_____

_____

_____

_____

A Geographer's World

MAIN IDEA

1. Maps and globes are the most commonly used tools of geographers.
2. Many geographers study information gathered by satellites.
3. Geographers use many other tools, including graphs, charts, databases, and models in their work.

Key Terms and Places

map flat drawing that shows part of Earth's surface

globe spherical model of the entire planet

Global Positioning System (GPS) tool that uses satellites to transmit locations of objects on Earth

Geographic Information System (GIS) information from many geographic data sources

Lesson Summary
MAPS AND GLOBES

Geographers need tools to do their work. Often, they use maps and globes. A **map** is a flat drawing that shows Earth's surface. A **globe** is a spherical (round) model of the whole planet.

Maps and globes both show what Earth looks like. Because a globe is round, it can show Earth as it really is. To show the round Earth on a flat map, some details have to change. For example, a place's shape may change a little. But maps have benefits. They are easier to work with. They can also show small areas, such as cities, better.

> Underline two sentences that tell the benefits of using maps.

SATELLITES

Geographers also use images and information from satellites. These images help geographers see what Earth looks like from far above.

Satellites are part of a **Global Positioning System (GPS).** This system uses 24 satellites to transmit information about locations of objects on Earth. Many people use GPS in their cars to find out how to get to a new place.

> Why do drivers use GPS in their cars?
>
> _____
>
> _____
>
> _____

OTHER GEOGRAPHIC TOOLS

Geographers use many other tools, including notebooks and voice recorders to take notes. They also work with computers, which lets them use a **Geographic Information System (GIS).** GIS makes it possible to get information from many data sources.

Geographers can ask GIS a question such as, "What are the most important geographic characteristics of an airport site?" GIS answers the question with different kinds of information, including maps.

> Circle the tools geographers use to take notes.

CHALLENGE ACTIVITY

Critical Thinking: Develop Pick a city you would like to study. You want to develop the most complete picture possible of this place and its people. Make a list of questions to ask and tools you would use to find the answers.

DIRECTIONS Circle the word or statement that relates most closely to the vocabulary word.

1. **globe:** spherical, city streets, drawing

2. **map:** entire planet, changed shapes, round

3. **Global Positioning System (GPS):** close-up images, satellites, regional languages

4. **Geographic Information System (GIS):** notebooks, driving directions, computer data

A Geographer's World

MAIN IDEAS
1. When creating maps, cartographers use a pattern of latitude and longitude lines that circle Earth.
2. Cartographers have created map projections to show the round surface of Earth on a flat piece of paper.
3. Cartographers provide features to help users read maps.
4. There are different kinds of maps for different uses.
5. There are many kinds of landforms and other features on Earth.

Key Terms and Places

grid imaginary lines that circle Earth in east–west and north–south directions

latitude east–west lines in the grid

parallels lines of latitude

longitude north–south lines in the grid

meridians lines of longitude

degrees units of measurement that locate lines of latitude and longitude

minutes unit of measurement that is 1/60 of a degree

equator imaginary line that circles the globe halfway between the North and South Poles

prime meridian imaginary line that divides the globe into east and west halves

hemispheres northern and southern or eastern and western halves of the globe

continents seven large landmasses on Earth's surface

map projections ways that our round planet can be shown on a flat map

Lesson Summary
LATITUDE AND LONGITUDE

Geographers created a pattern of imaginary lines that circle the globe. These lines are called a **grid.** East–west lines are lines of **latitude.** They are also called **parallels** because they are always parallel to each other. North–south lines are called lines of **longitude,** or **meridians.** They pass through the poles.

> Why are lines of latitude called parallels?
>
> _____
>
> _____

The location of latitude and longitude is measured using **degrees,** or a ° symbol. Degrees are divided into 60 smaller measurements called **minutes.** Degrees and minutes help geographers locate any place on Earth.

Lines of latitude are north and south of the equator. The **equator** is an imaginary line that circles the globe halfway between the North and South Poles. Lines of longitude are east and west of an imaginary line called the **prime meridian.** The prime meridian divides the globe into east and west halves.

Lines of latitude start at 0° at the equator. North of the equator, they are labeled with an *N.* For example, the North Pole is located at 90°N. South of the equator, they are labeled with an *S.* The South Pole is located at 90°S.

Lines of longitude start at 0° at the prime meridian. They go up to 180°, which is the middle of the Pacific Ocean. Meridians west of the prime meridian to 180° are labeled with a *W.* Meridians east of the prime meridian to 180° are labeled with an *E.*

The equator and prime meridian divide the globe into **hemispheres,** or halves. The equator divides the world into the Northern Hemisphere and Southern Hemisphere. The prime meridian divides it into the Eastern Hemisphere and Western Hemisphere.

Earth's surface is further divided into seven large landmasses, called **continents.** Earth's major ocean region is divided into five smaller oceans.

> **Underline the sentence that states how degree measurements help geographers.**

> **What are the latitudes of the most northern and most southern points on Earth?**
>
> _____
>
> _____

> **Circle the imaginary line that divides the globe into Northern and Southern Hemispheres.**

MAP PROJECTIONS

Mapmakers use **map projections** to show our round planet on a flat map. All flat maps are distorted in some way. Mapmakers use one of three map projections: cylindrical, conic, or flat-plane.

Cylindrical projections are based on a cylinder wrapped around a globe at the equator. These maps pull the meridians apart so they are parallel to each other and do not meet at the poles. This makes the land areas at the poles look larger.

Conic projections are based on a cone placed over a globe. It is most accurate along the lines of latitude where the cone touches the globe.

Flat-plane projections are based on a flat shape touching the globe at only one point, such as the North Pole. It shows true direction and true area. That can help navigators. However, it distorts the shapes of land areas.

> Circle the three types of map projections.

> Underline the sentence that explains why navigators might want to use a flat-planed map.

MAP FEATURES

Most maps include four features that help us understand them and what they present. The first feature we usually see is a title. The map title tells you what the map is trying to show. Another feature is a compass rose. This has arrows that show which way north, south, east, and west lie on the map. A third feature is a scale. It is used to measure the distance between points on a map. The fourth important feature is a legend. It explains what symbols and colors represent on the map. For example, roads might be different colors, showing whether they are highways or two lanes.

Some maps include a locator map as a fifth feature. This shows where the area on the map is located in the larger world.

> Circle the four features you are likely to find on most maps.

Guided Reading Workbook

DIFFERENT KINDS OF MAPS

Political and physical maps are two of the most common maps, but there are also many types of thematic maps. Political maps use different colors to show borders of countries, capital cities, and other places in a region. Physical maps show features like mountain ranges, rivers, and deserts in a region. They often use different colors to represent different elevations. Thematic maps focus on one topic, like climate, resources, or population. They may show the information using different colors, arrows, or other symbols.

> **Name three kinds of thematic maps.**
>
> _____
>
> _____
>
> _____

EARTH'S SURFACE FEATURES

Landforms are features on Earth's surface that are formed by nature. There are many kinds of landforms and water features on Earth. Landform features include hills, valleys, and mountains, while water features include oceans, rivers, and lakes.

CHALLENGE ACTIVITY

Critical Thinking: Design a Map Create a small map of your school. Add a title, compass rose, scale, and legend to explain what the map is about and how to understand its colors and symbols.

DIRECTIONS On the line provided before each statement, write **T** if the statement is true and **F** if the statement is false. If the statement is false, write the correct answer on the line after each sentence that makes the sentence a true statement.

_____ 1. Lines of <u>longitude</u> are also called <u>meridians</u>.

_____

_____ 2. Geographers created a <u>grid</u> to help find locations on the globe.

_____

_____ 3. <u>Minutes</u> are divided in smaller units called <u>degrees</u>.

_____

_____ 4. Lines of <u>latitude</u> meet at the poles.

_____

_____ 5. The <u>equator</u> divides the globe into a Northern <u>Hemisphere</u> and a Southern Hemisphere.

_____

_____ 6. The location of the <u>prime meridian</u> is 0°.

_____

_____ 7. Lines of <u>latitude</u> run in parallel east–west paths around the globe.

_____

_____ 8. Mapmakers use a <u>compass rose</u> to show our round planet on a flat map.

_____

_____ 9. The seven large landmasses on Earth's surface are called <u>continents</u>.

_____

Guided Reading Workbook

The Physical World

MAIN IDEAS

1. Earth's movement affects the amount of energy we receive from the sun.
2. Earth's seasons are caused by the planet's tilt.

Key Terms and Places

solar energy energy from the sun

rotation one complete spin of Earth on its axis

revolution one trip of Earth around the sun

tropics regions close to the equator

Lesson Summary
EARTH'S MOVEMENT

Energy from the sun, or **solar energy,** is necessary for life on Earth. It helps plants grow and provides light and heat. Several factors affect the amount of solar energy Earth receives. These are rotation, revolution, tilt, and latitude.

Earth's axis is an imaginary rod running from the North Pole to the South Pole. Earth spins around on its axis. One complete **rotation** takes 24 hours, or one day. It looks as if the sun is moving, but it is really the planet's rotation that creates that effect.

Solar energy reaches only half of the planet at a time. The half that faces the sun receives light and warmth, creating daytime. In the half that faces away from the sun, it is nighttime, which is darker and cooler.

As Earth rotates, it also moves around the sun. It takes Earth a year, 365 1/4 days, to complete one **revolution** around the sun. Every four years, an extra day is added to February. This makes up for the extra quarter of a day.

Earth's axis is tilted, not straight up and down. At different times of year, some locations tilt toward

---

> List the four factors that affect the amount of solar energy Earth receives.
>
> _____
>
> _____

> What would happen if Earth did not rotate?
>
> _____
>
> _____
>
> _____

> Underline the sentence that describes Earth's revolution around the sun.

Guided Reading Workbook

the sun. They get more solar energy than
locations tilted away from the sun.

Latitude refers to imaginary lines that run east
and west around the planet, north and south of
Earth's equator. Areas near the equator receive
direct rays from the sun all year and have warm
temperatures. Higher latitudes receive fewer
direct rays and are cooler.

> **Why are areas near the equator warmer than those in higher latitudes?**
>
> _____
>
> _____

THE SEASONS

Many locations on Earth have four seasons:
winter, spring, summer, and fall. These are based
on temperature and how long the days are.

The seasons change because of the tilt of
Earth's axis. In summer, the Northern
Hemisphere is tilted toward the sun. It receives
more solar energy than during the winter, when it
is tilted away from the sun.

Because Earth's axis is tilted, the hemispheres
have opposite seasons. Winter in the Northern
Hemisphere is summer in the Southern
Hemisphere. During the fall and spring, the poles
point neither toward nor away from the sun. In
spring, temperatures rise and days become longer
as summer approaches. In fall, the opposite
occurs.

> **What would the seasons be like in the Northern and Southern Hemispheres if Earth's axis weren't tilted?**
>
> _____
>
> _____

In some regions, the seasons are tied to rainfall
instead of temperature. One of these regions,
close to the equator, is the **tropics.** There, winds
bring heavy rains from June to October. The
weather turns dry in the tropics from November
to January.

> **Circle the name of the warm region near the equator.**

CHALLENGE ACTIVITY

Critical Thinking: Draw Conclusions Imagine that
you are a travel agent. One of your clients is
planning a trip to Argentina in June, and another
is planning a trip to Chicago in August. What
kinds of clothing would you suggest they pack
for their trips and why?

| latitude | rainfall | revolution |
| rotation | solar energy | tropics |

DIRECTIONS On the line provided before each statement, write **T** if a statement is true and **F** if a statement is false. If the statement is false, write the term from the word bank that would make the statement correct on the line after each sentence.

_____ 1. The hemisphere of Earth that is tilted away from the sun receives less direct <u>rainfall</u> than the other hemisphere receives.

_____

_____ 2. An umbrella might be more useful to a person in the <u>tropics</u> than a winter coat.

_____

_____ 3. Earth's path, or orbit, around the sun is its <u>rotation</u>.

_____

_____ 4. One <u>revolution</u> of Earth takes 24 hours.

_____

_____ 5. Plants in an area of high latitude receive less direct solar energy during the year than plants at a <u>lower latitude</u> because they are farther from the equator.

_____

The Physical World

MAIN IDEAS

1. Salt water and freshwater make up Earth's water supply.
2. In the water cycle, water circulates from Earth's surface to the atmosphere and back again.
3. Water plays an important role in people's lives.

Key Terms and Places

freshwater water without salt

glaciers large areas of slow-moving ice

surface water water that is stored in Earth's streams, rivers, and lakes

precipitation water that falls to Earth's surface as rain, snow, sleet, or hail

groundwater water found below Earth's surface

water vapor water that occurs in the air as an invisible gas

water cycle the circulation of water from Earth's surface to the atmosphere and back

Lesson Summary
EARTH'S WATER SUPPLY

Approximately two-thirds of Earth's surface is covered with water. There are two kinds of water: salt water and **freshwater.** About 97 percent of Earth's water is salt water. Most of it is in the oceans, seas, gulfs, bays, and straits. Some lakes, such as the Great Salt Lake in Utah, also contain salt water.

Salt water cannot be used for drinking. Only freshwater is safe to drink. Freshwater is found in lakes and rivers and stored underground. Much is frozen in the ice found in **glaciers,** as well as the Arctic and Antarctic regions.

One form of freshwater is **surface water.** This is stored in streams, lakes, and rivers. Streams form when **precipitation** falls to Earth as rain, snow, sleet, or hail. These streams then flow into larger

> Circle the places where we find salt water.

> Underline the places where we find freshwater.

streams and rivers. Less than 1 percent of Earth's water supply comes from surface water.

Most freshwater is stored underground. **Groundwater** bubbles to the surface in springs or can be reached by digging deep holes, or wells.

THE WATER CYCLE

Water is the only substance on Earth that can take the form of a liquid, gas, or solid. In its solid form, water is snow and ice. Liquid water is rain or water found in lakes and rivers. **Water vapor** is an invisible form of water in the air.

> Underline the words that define water vapor.

Water is always moving. When water on Earth's surface heats up, it evaporates and turns into water vapor. It then rises from Earth into the atmosphere. When it cools down, it changes from water vapor to liquid. Droplets of water form clouds. When they get heavier, these droplets fall to Earth as precipitation. This process of evaporation and precipitation is called the **water cycle.**

> What are the two main processes of the water cycle?
> _____
> _____

Some precipitation is absorbed into the soil as groundwater. The rest flows into streams, rivers, and oceans.

WATER AND PEOPLE

Water is crucial for survival. It is a problem when people lack freshwater because of shortages. Shortages are caused by overuse and by drought, when there is little or no precipitation for a long time. Water shortages can lead to less food. Another problem is pollution. Chemicals and waste can pollute water, making it dangerous to use. Lack of water can lead to conflicts when countries fight over who controls water supplies.

> Circle two words that are causes of water shortages.

Water can affect the physical environment. For example, sinkholes are formed when water dissolves the surface layer of the ground. Heavy rains can cause flooding that damages property and threatens lives.

> How does water cause sinkholes?
> _____
> _____

Water has many benefits, too. It quenches our thirst and allows us to have food to eat. Flowing water is an important source of electric energy. Water also provides recreation, making our lives richer and more enjoyable.

Water is essential for life on Earth. Cities and even nations are now working together to manage freshwater supplies. For example, Central Florida Water Initiative works with businesses and many other groups to protect the water resources in that region.

> **How does the Central Florida Water Initiative help water supplies?**
> _____
> _____
> _____
> _____
> _____

CHALLENGE ACTIVITY

Critical Thinking: Solve Problems You are campaigning for public office. Write a speech describing three actions you plan to take to protect supplies of freshwater.

DIRECTIONS Read each sentence, and fill in the blank with the word in the word pair that best completes the sentence.

1. Some freshwater is locked in Earth's _____. (**water vapor/ glaciers**)

2. Less than 1 percent of Earth's water supply comes from _____ stored in streams, rivers, and lakes. (**surface water/ groundwater**)

3. Water can be a solid (ice), a liquid, or a gas called _____. (**precipitation/water vapor**)

4. The water brought to the surface from deep holes is _____. (**freshwater/groundwater**)

5. _____ is water that falls from clouds as rain, snow, sleet, or hail. (**Precipitation/Water cycle**)

6. Surface water is a form of _____. (**glacier/freshwater**)

freshwater	glacier	groundwater	precipitation
surface water	water cycle	water vapor	

DIRECTIONS Use the terms from the word bank to write a summary of what you learned in the lesson.

_____

_____

_____

_____

_____

_____

_____

The Physical World

Lesson 3

MAIN IDEAS
1. Earth's surface is covered by many different landforms.
2. Forces below Earth's surface build up our landforms.
3. Forces on the planet's surface shape Earth's landforms.
4. Landforms influence people's lives and culture.

Key Terms and Places

landforms shapes on Earth's surface, such as hills or mountains

continents large landmasses

plate tectonics theory suggesting that Earth's surface is divided into more than 12 slow-moving plates, or pieces of Earth's crust

lava magma, or liquid rock, that reaches Earth's surface

earthquakes sudden, violent movements of Earth's crust

weathering process of breaking rock into smaller pieces

erosion movement of sediment from one location to another

alluvial deposition process by which rivers create floodplains and deltas when they flood and deposit sediment along the banks

Lesson Summary

LANDFORMS

Geographers study **landforms** such as mountains, valleys, plains, islands, and peninsulas. They study how landforms are made and how they affect human activity.

> **Give two examples of landforms.**
> _____
> _____
> _____

FORCES BELOW EARTH'S SURFACE

The planet is made up of three layers. Below the top layer, or crust, is a layer of liquid. Earth's center, the third layer, is a solid core. The planet has seven **continents,** large landmasses that are part of Earth's crust. Earth's crust is divided into 12 pieces, called plates. These plates move very slowly. Geographers have a theory called **plate tectonics,** which explains how plates' movements shape our landforms.

> **What are plates?**
> _____
> _____

Energy from deep inside the planet makes the plates move at different speeds and in different directions. As they move, they shift the continents. This is known as continental drift. Plates move in three ways: they collide, they separate, and they slide past each other.

> **Underline the sentence that lists the three different ways in which Earth's plates move.**

The energy of colliding plates creates new landforms. When two ocean plates collide, they may form deep valleys on the ocean's floor. When ocean plates collide with continental plates, mountain ranges are formed. Mountains are also created when two continental plates collide.

> **Underline what happens when two ocean plates collide with one another.**

When plates separate, usually on the ocean floor, they cause gaps in the planet's crust. Magma, or liquid rock, rises through the cracks as **lava.** As it cools, it forms underwater mountains or ridges. Sometimes these mountains rise above the surface of the water and form islands.

Plates can also slide past each other. When they grind past each other, they cause **earthquakes.** Earthquakes often happen along faults, or breaks in Earth's crust.

> **What causes earthquakes?**
> _____
> _____

PROCESSES ON EARTH'S SURFACE

As landforms are created, other forces work to wear them away. **Weathering** breaks larger rocks into smaller rocks. Changes in temperature can cause cracks in rocks. Water then gets into the cracks, expands as it freezes, and breaks the rocks. Rocks eventually break down into smaller pieces called sediment.

Another force that wears down landforms is **erosion.** Erosion takes place when sediment is moved by water, ice, and wind. The most common cause of erosion is water. Rivers can flood their banks and deposit sediment, a process called **alluvial deposition.** This creates floodplains and river deltas.

> **Circle the three elements that cause erosion.**

LANDFORMS INFLUENCE LIFE

Landforms influence where people live. For example, people might want to farm in an area with good soil and water. Mineral deposits may create jobs in mining. People also change landforms in many ways. For example, engineers build tunnels through mountains to make roads. Farmers build terraces on steep hillsides.

CHALLENGE ACTIVITY

Critical Thinking: Draw Inferences Find out about a landform in your area that was changed by people. Write a report explaining why and how it was changed.

DIRECTIONS Look at each set of four vocabulary terms. On the line provided, write the letter of the term that does not relate to the others.

_____ 1. a. erosion   b. weathering   c. landform   d. continent

_____ 2. a. lava   b. alluvial depositions   c. earthquake   d. plate tectonics

alluvial depositions	continents	earthquake	erosion
landforms	lava	plate tectonics	weathering

DIRECTIONS Answer each question by writing a sentence that contains at least one word from the word bank.

3. What are two ways that the movements of tectonic plates affect Earth?

_____

_____

4. What is the most common cause of erosion?

_____

_____

DIRECTIONS Choose four of the terms from the word bank. Look them up in a dictionary. Write the definition of the word that is closest to the definition that is used in your textbook.

_____

_____

_____

_____

The Physical World

MAIN IDEAS

1. While weather is short term, climate is a region's average weather over a long period.
2. The amount of sun at a given location is affected by Earth's tilt, movement, and shape.
3. Wind and water move heat around Earth, affecting how warm or wet a place is.
4. Mountains influence temperature and precipitation.

Key Terms and Places

weather short-term changes in the air for a given place and time

climate region's average weather conditions over a long period

prevailing winds winds that blow in the same direction over large areas of Earth

ocean currents large streams of surface seawater

front place where two air masses of different temperature or moisture content meet

Lesson Summary

UNDERSTANDING WEATHER AND CLIMATE

Weather is the temperature and precipitation at a specific time and place. **Climate** is a region's average weather over a long period of time. Climate and weather are affected by the sun, location on Earth, wind, water, and mountains.

> Circle the forces that affect climate and weather.

SUN AND LOCATION

The parts of Earth tilted toward the sun get more solar energy than the parts tilted away from the sun. This changes during the year, creating seasons. While some locations are having a warm summer, others are having a cold winter.

Energy from the sun falls more directly on the equator, so that area has warm temperatures all year. It gets colder as you move away from the low latitude of the equator. The coldest areas are at the poles, the highest latitudes.

> Underline the sentence that explains why the equator has warm temperatures year-round.

Lesson 4, *continued*

WIND AND WATER

Heat from the sun moves around Earth, partly because of winds. Winds blow in great streams around the planet. They are caused by the rising and sinking of air. Cold air sinks and warm air rises. More air flows in to take the place of the air that has moved.

Prevailing winds are winds that blow in the same direction over large areas of Earth. Hot air rises at the equator and flows toward the poles. Cold air at the poles sinks and moves toward the equator. The planet's rotation curves the winds east or west. Prevailing winds control an area's climate. They make regions warmer or colder, drier or wetter. They pick up moisture from water and dry out as they pass over land.

Large bodies of water also affect temperature. **Ocean currents** are large streams of surface water that carry warm water from the equator toward the poles and cold water from the poles toward the equator. Water heats and cools more slowly than land. Therefore, water helps to moderate the temperature of nearby land, keeping it from getting very hot or very cold.

Storms happen when two large bodies of air collide. A **front** is a place where two air masses with different temperatures or moisture collide. In the United States and other regions, warm and cold air masses meet often, causing severe weather. These can include thunderstorms, blizzards, and tornadoes. Tornadoes are twisting funnels of air that touch the ground. Hurricanes are large tropical storms that form over water. They bring strong winds and heavy rain. Tornadoes and hurricanes are both dangerous and destructive.

> **What causes wind?**
> _____
> _____

> **Which heats and cools more slowly—land or water?**
> _____

> **What often happens when warm and cold air masses meet?**
> _____
> _____
> _____

MOUNTAINS

Mountains also affect climate. The higher areas are colder than the lower elevations. Warm air blowing against a mountainside rises and cools. Clouds form, and precipitation falls on the side facing the wind. However, there is little moisture on the other side of the mountain. This effect creates a rain shadow, a dry area on the side of the mountain facing away from the direction of the wind.

> **Which areas are colder— lower or higher elevations?**
> _____

CHALLENGE ACTIVITY

Critical Thinking: Sequence Write a short description of the process leading up to the formation of a rain shadow. Draw and label a picture to go with your description.

DIRECTIONS On the line provided before each statement, write **T** if a statement is true and **F** if a statement is false. If the statement is false, write the correct term on the line after each sentence that makes the sentence true.

_____ 1. <u>Climate</u> describes the atmospheric conditions in a place at a specific time. It changes rapidly.

_____

_____

_____ 2. <u>Precipitation</u> falls on the side of a mountain that faces the wind.

_____

_____ 3. <u>Fronts</u> may form when air masses of different temperatures come together.

_____

_____ 4. <u>Ocean currents</u> affect the temperature of nearby land.

_____

_____ 5. Warm air at the <u>poles</u> rises, causing prevailing winds that travel toward the <u>equator</u>.

_____

_____

climate	equator	front	ocean currents
poles	precipitation	prevailing winds	weather

DIRECTIONS Choose five of the vocabulary words from the word bank. On a separate sheet of paper, use these words to write a summary of what you learned in the lesson.

_____

_____

_____

_____

_____

The Physical World

MAIN IDEAS
1. Geographers use temperature, precipitation, and plant life to identify climate zones.
2. Tropical climates are wet and warm, while dry climates receive little or no rain.
3. Temperate climates have the most seasonal change.
4. Polar climates are cold and dry, while highland climates change with elevation.

Key Terms and Places

monsoons winds that shift direction with the seasons and create wet and dry periods

savannas areas of tall grasses and scattered trees and shrubs

steppes semidry grasslands or prairies

permafrost permanently frozen layers of soil

Lesson Summary
MAJOR CLIMATE ZONES

We can divide Earth into five climate zones: tropical, temperate, polar, dry, and highland. Tropical climates appear near the equator, temperate climates are found in the middle latitudes, and polar climates occur near the poles. Dry and highland climates can appear at different latitudes.

> Underline the names of the five climate zones.

TROPICAL AND DRY CLIMATES

Humid tropical climates occur near the equator. Some are hot and humid throughout the year. Rain forests need this type of climate to thrive and support thousands of species. Other tropical areas have **monsoons**—winds that shift directions and create wet and dry seasons.

Moving away from the equator, we find tropical savanna climates. A long, hot dry season is followed by short periods of rain. This climate supports **savannas,** an area of tall grasses and scattered trees and shrubs.

> What happens when monsoon winds change direction?
>
> _____
> _____

Deserts are hot and dry. At night, the dry air cools quickly; desert nights can be cold. Only a few tough plants and animals survive in a desert. Sometimes **steppes**—semidry grasslands—are found near deserts.

TEMPERATE CLIMATES

Temperate, or mild, climates occur in the middle latitudes. In this climate, weather often changes quickly when cold and warm air masses meet. Most temperate regions have four distinct seasons, with hot summers and cold winters.

A Mediterranean climate has hot, sunny summers and mild, wet winters. They occur near the ocean, and the climate is mostly pleasant. People like to vacation in these climates. Only small, scattered trees survive in these areas.

East coasts near the tropics have humid subtropical climates because winds bring moisture from the ocean. They have hot, wet summers and mild winters, with storms year-round. Marine west coast climates occur farther north on the west coast. They also get moisture from the sea, which causes mild summers and rainy winters. Inland or east-coast regions in the upper-middle latitudes often have humid continental climates. These have short, hot summers, a mild spring and fall, and long, cold winters.

POLAR AND HIGHLAND CLIMATES

There are three polar climates. Subarctic climate occurs south of the Arctic Ocean. Winters are long and very cold; summers are cool. There is enough precipitation to support forests. At the same latitude near the coasts, tundra climate is also cold, but too dry for trees to survive. In parts of the tundra, soil is frozen as **permafrost.**

> Circle the name of the climate that can have four distinct seasons.

> What do people typically like to do in Mediterranean climates?
> _____

> What kind of climate do you live in?
> _____
> _____
> _____

> Can there be forests in subarctic climates? Explain.
> _____
> _____
> _____

Ice cap climates are the coldest on Earth. There is little precipitation and little vegetation. Even though it is a harsh place, penguins and polar bears live there.

Highland, or mountain, climate changes with elevation. As you go up a mountain, the climate may go from tropical to polar.

CHALLENGE ACTIVITY
Critical Thinking: Compare and Contrast
Create a table showing the differences and similarities between any two types of climate.

DIRECTIONS Write three words or phrases that describe the term.

1. savanna _____

2. steppe _____

3. monsoon _____

_____

4. permafrost _____

_____

DIRECTIONS Look at each set of four terms. On the line provided, write the letter of the term that does not relate to the others.

_____ 5. a. humid continental
        b. marine west coast
        c. Mediterranean
        d. steppe

_____ 6. a. subarctic
        b. tundra
        c. desert
        d. permafrost

_____ 7. a. monsoon
        b. muggy
        c. prairies
        d. rain forest

_____ 8. a. forest
        b. steppes
        c. savannas
        d. grassland

The Physical World

MAIN IDEAS
1. The environment and life are interconnected and exist in a fragile balance.
2. Soils play an important role in the environment.

Key Terms and Places

environment plant or animal's surroundings

ecosystem any place where plants and animals depend upon each other and their environment for survival

biome area much larger than an ecosystem and possibly made up of several ecosystems

habitat place where a plant or animal lives

extinct to die out completely

humus decayed plant or animal matter

desertification slow process of losing soil fertility and plant life

Lesson Summary
THE ENVIRONMENT AND LIFE

Plants and animals cannot live just anywhere. They must have an **environment**, or surroundings, that suits them. Climate, land features, and water are all part of a living thing's environment. Plants and animals adapt to specific environments. For example, kangaroo rats do not need to drink much water and are adapted to a desert environment.

An **ecosystem** is the connection between a particular environment and the plants and animals that live there. They all depend on each other for survival. Ecosystems can be as small as a garden pond or as large as a forest. **Biomes** are much larger than ecosystems. They may contain several ecosystems.

Each part of an ecosystem fills a certain role in a cycle. For example, the sun provides energy to plants, which use it to make food. These plants

> Which is larger, a biome or an ecosystem?
>
> _____

> Underline the sentences that describe the steps in an ecosystem's cycle.

then provide energy and food to other plants and animals. When these life forms die, their bodies break down and give nutrients to the soil so more plants can grow.

A small change in one part of an ecosystem can affect the whole system. Many natural events and human actions affect ecosystems and the habitats in them. A **habitat** is the place where a plant or animal lives. Natural events include forest fires, disease, and climate changes.

> **Circle the natural events that can affect ecosystems.**

Human actions such as clearing land and polluting can destroy habitats. For example, people are clearing Earth's rain forests for farmland, lumber, and other reasons. As a result, these diverse habitats are being lost. If a change to the environment is extreme, a species might become **extinct,** or die out completely.

> **What two human actions are destroying habitats?**
>
> _____
>
> _____

Many countries are passing laws to protect the environment. Although these laws do not please everyone, they can have good results. The U.S. Endangered Species Act of 1973 has saved 47 species from becoming extinct.

SOIL AND THE ENVIRONMENT

An environment's soil affects which plants can grow there. Fertile soils have lots of humus and minerals. **Humus** is decayed plant or animal matter.

> **Circle two things found in fertile soil.**

Soils can lose fertility from erosion when wind or water sweeps topsoil away. Soil can also lose fertility from planting the same crops repeatedly. When soil becomes worn out and can no longer support plants, **desertification** can occur. The spread of desert conditions causes problems in many parts of the world.

CHALLENGE ACTIVITY

Critical Thinking: Draw Inferences Consider the interconnections in your environment. As you go through a normal day, keep a list of the sources you rely on for energy, food, and water.

DIRECTIONS Read each sentence and fill in the blank with the word in the word pair that best completes the sentence.

1. Organic material called _____ enriches the soil. **(biomes/humus)**

2. When soil gets worn out, it may lead to _____. **(erosion/desertification)**

3. A rainforest is a/an _____, which can contain many different ecosystems. **(biome/environment)**

4. If there are too many changes in conditions, a species may die out, or become _____. **(consequence/extinct)**

5. Plants and animals are adapted to the specific _____ where they live. **(environment/humus)**

6. Laws have been passed to protect _____ from human activities that could destroy them. **(habitats/nutrients)**

biome	desertification	ecosystem	environment
erosion	extinct	fertile soils	habitat
humus	nutrients		

DIRECTIONS Choose five of the words from the word bank. On a separate sheet of paper, use these words to write a poem or story that relates to the lesson.

The Physical World

MAIN IDEAS
1. Earth provides valuable resources for our use.
2. Energy resources provide fuel, heat, and electricity.
3. Mineral resources include metals, rocks, and salt.
4. Resources shape people's lives and countries' wealth.

Key Terms and Places

natural resource any material in nature that people use and value

renewable resources resources that can be replaced naturally

nonrenewable resources resources that cannot be replaced

deforestation loss of forestland

reforestation planting trees to replace lost forestland

fossil fuels nonrenewable resources formed from the remains of ancient plants and animals

hydroelectric power production of electricity by moving water

Lesson Summary
EARTH'S VALUABLE RESOURCES

Anything in nature that people use and value is a **natural resource.** Earth's most important natural resources are air, water, soils, forests, and minerals. We often use these resources to make something new. For example, we make paper from trees. Resources such as trees are called **renewable resources** because another tree can grow in its place. Resources that cannot be replaced, such as oil, are called **nonrenewable resources.**

Even though forests are renewable, we can cut down trees faster than they can grow. For example, in Brazil, illegal logging is destroying rain forests. The loss of forests is called **deforestation.** When we plant trees to replace lost forests, we call it **reforestation.**

> Circle the natural resources that are most important.

> Underline the sentence that explains why there is deforestation even though trees are renewable resources.

Guided Reading Workbook

ENERGY RESOURCES

Most of our energy comes from **fossil fuels,** which are formed from the remains of ancient living things. These include coal, oil, and natural gas.

We use coal mostly for electricity, but it causes air pollution. Since there is a lot of coal, people are trying to find cleaner ways to use it. Another fossil fuel is petroleum, or oil. It is used to make different kinds of fuels and heating oil. Oil can also be turned into plastics, cosmetics, and other products.

> Circle four products made from oil.

We depend on fossil fuels for much of our energy, so they are very valuable. However, fuel from oil can cause air and land pollution. Oil spills pollute the water and hurt wildlife. The cleanest fossil fuel is natural gas, which is used mainly for cooking and heating.

> What is the cleanest-burning fossil fuel?
> _____

Many scientists believe that burning fossil fuels causes climate change. They believe Earth's temperature is rising. More than 190 countries have signed the Kyoto Protocol, an agreement adopted in 1997 that sets targets to reduce emissions from burning fossil fuels. They hope this will reduce pollution from fossil fuels.

Renewable energy resources include **hydroelectric power**—the creation of electricity from the motion and movement of running water. This is accomplished mainly by building dams on rivers. Other renewable energy sources are wind and solar energy. Wind produces electricity with windmills, and solar energy uses the power of sunlight to generate electricity.

> Underline the sentence that explains why some people do not want to use nuclear energy.

One nonrenewable resource is nuclear energy. This type of energy is created by splitting atoms, small particles of matter. Although nuclear energy does not pollute the air, it does produce dangerous waste material that must be stored for thousands of years.

MINERAL RESOURCES

Like oil, minerals are nonrenewable and can be very valuable. Minerals include metals, salt, rocks, and gemstones. Minerals like iron are used to make steel. We make buildings from stone and window glass from quartz. We also use minerals to make jewelry, coins, and many other common objects. Recycling minerals like aluminum in cans can make these resources last longer.

```
┌─────────────────────────┐
│ List four uses of minerals. │
│ ─────────────────────── │
│ ─────────────────────── │
│ ─────────────────────── │
└─────────────────────────┘
```

RESOURCES AND PEOPLE

Natural resources vary from place to place. Some places are rich in natural resources. Resources such as fertile farmland, forests, and oil have helped the United States become a powerful country with a strong economy. Places with fewer resources do not have the wealth and choices of Americans.

Some countries use their resources to trade for resources they do not have. For example, many Middle Eastern countries are rich in oil but do not have water to grow food. They must use their oil profits to import food. Some of these countries are part of The Organization of the Petroleum Exporting Countries (OPEC). This group of 13 countries helps control oil prices so oil-producing countries can use the wealth to buy products they need.

```
┌─────────────────────────┐
│ What is OPEC?           │
│ ─────────────────────── │
│ ─────────────────────── │
│ ─────────────────────── │
└─────────────────────────┘
```

CHALLENGE ACTIVITY

Critical Thinking: Draw Inferences Write a short essay explaining how America's natural resources have helped it become a powerful country.

deforestation	electricity	fossil fuels
hydroelectric power	natural resources	nonrenewable resources
petroleum	reforestation	renewable resources

DIRECTIONS Answer each question by writing a sentence that contains at least one word from the word bank.

1. What problem is caused when trees are cut down faster than they can grow back? How can this problem be fixed?

_____

_____

_____

2. What are some examples of energy resources we can use instead of fossil fuels? List two types, and explain how they work.

_____

_____

_____

3. What may happen to a country that has only a few natural resources?

_____

_____

_____

DIRECTIONS Write three examples of each term.

4. natural resources _____

5. renewable resources _____

6. fossil fuels _____

The Human World

MAIN IDEAS
1. Culture is the set of beliefs, goals, and practices that a group of people share.
2. The world includes many different culture groups.
3. New ideas and events lead to changes in culture.
4. The features common to all cultures are called cultural universals.
5. All societies have social institutions that help their groups survive.
6. Every culture expresses itself creatively in a variety of ways.
7. All societies use technology to help shape and control the environment.

Key Terms and Places

culture set of beliefs, values, and practices a group of people have in common

culture trait activity or behavior in which people often take part

culture region area in which people have many shared culture traits

ethnic group group of people who share a common culture and ancestry

multicultural society society that includes a variety of cultures in the same area

cultural diffusion spread of culture traits from one region to another

cultural universals features societies have developed that are common to all cultures

social institutions organized patterns of belief and behavior that focus on meeting societal needs

heritage wealth of cultural elements that has been passed down over generations

universal theme message about life or human nature that is meaningful across time and in all places

technology use of knowledge, tools, and skills to solve problems

Lesson Summary
WHAT IS CULTURE?

Culture is the set of beliefs, values, and practices a group of people have in common. Everything in day-to-day life is part of culture, including language, religion, clothes, music, and foods.

> Underline the sentence that lists some examples of culture.

People everywhere share certain basic cultural features, such as forming a government, educating children, and creating art or music. However, people practice these things in different ways, making each culture unique.

Culture traits are activities or behaviors in which people often take part, such as language and popular sports. People share some culture traits but not others. For example, people eat using forks, chopsticks, or their fingers in different areas.

Cultures are often passed from one generation to the next. They may be based on family traditions, like holiday customs, or laws and moral codes passed down within a society. Other factors that influence how cultures develop include immigrants moving to a new country, historical events, and the environment where people live and work.

> **What are three factors that influence how a culture develops?**
>
> _____
> _____
> _____
> _____

CULTURE GROUPS

There are thousands of different cultures in the world. People who share a culture are part of a culture group that may be based on things like age or religion.

A **culture region** is an area in which people have many shared culture traits such as language, religion, or lifestyle. A cultural region can extend over many countries. For example, most people in North Africa and Southeast Asia share the Arabic language and Muslim religion. Some countries, like Japan, may be a single culture region. Other countries may have several different culture regions.

> **Circle the country that is also a single cultural region.**

Often, cultural regions within a country are based on ethnic groups. An **ethnic group** is a group of people who often share cultural traits like language, foods, or religion. Sometimes, though, people who have the same religion are still in different ethnic groups, and different ethnic groups can have different religious beliefs.

Countries or areas with many ethnic groups are **multicultural societies**. Multiculturalism can create an interesting mix of ideas and practices, but it can also lead to conflict. In Canada, French Canadians want to separate from the rest of Canada. In Rwanda, a 1990s ethnic conflict led to extreme violence. In some countries, like the U.S., different ethnic groups cooperate and live side by side. That is because so many people have migrated to the country from all over the world and they celebrate their ethnic heritage.

> **Why are different ethnic groups likely to cooperate in the U.S.?**
> _____
> _____
> _____
> _____
> _____

CHANGES IN CULTURE

Cultures change constantly, sometimes quickly and sometimes over years. Two main causes of change are new ideas or contact with other societies. New technology like motion pictures and the Internet have changed how people spend their time and how they communicate. Contact with another culture may cause both to change. For example, both Spanish and Native American cultures changed when the Spanish arrived in the Americas.

> **Underline two sentences that describe examples that cause cultures to change.**

Cultural diffusion is the spread of culture traits from one part of the world to another. It occurs when people bring their culture to another country. This happens when people immigrate or when people trade goods in different regions. People also move to other countries to escape conflicts and wars.

> **What are three ways cultural diffusion occurs?**
> _____
> _____
> _____
> _____

WHAT DO ALL CULTURES HAVE IN COMMON?

All people have the same basic needs, such as food, clothing, and shelter. Geographers believe that all societies have developed **cultural universals**—specific features that meet basic needs. Three important cultural universals are social institutions, creative expressions, and technology.

· Guided Reading Workbook

BASIC SOCIAL INSTITUTIONS

Social institutions are organized patterns of belief and behavior that focus on meeting the needs of the society's members. The most basic social institutions are family, education, religion, government, and economy. These institutions are shaped by a group's cultural values and principles, which vary from culture to culture.

Family is the most basic social institution. The family cares for the children and provides support. They also teach the culture's values and traditions, often through elders. Family members may live together under one roof or be part of a whole village. Societies also pass on values and knowledge through education. For example, U.S. schools teach students how to be good citizens.

Although there are many religions, they all help explain the meanings of life and death and the difference between good and bad behavior. Religions' practices and traditions make them the source of many cultures' beliefs and attitudes. In all world regions, religion has inspired great works of devotion, including art and architecture.

Government is a system of leaders and laws that help people live together in their community or country. It defines standards, protects property and people's rights, and helps settle conflicts. A society's economy is its system of using resources to meet needs. Economic principles guide the way a nation does business.

> **Circle the most basic social institutions.**

> **What do all religions have in common?**
> _____
> _____
> _____
> _____
> _____
> _____
> _____
> _____

CREATIVE EXPRESSIONS

Societies, like individuals, express themselves creatively. There are three main types of creative expression. Performing arts include music, theater, and dance. Visual arts include painting, sculpture, and architecture. Literary arts are related in words and language such as literature and folklore.

> **What are the three main types of creative expressions?**
> _____
> _____

Creative expressions reflect a specific **heritage,** or wealth of cultural elements that have been passed down through generations. Creative expressions also express individual choices, as well as universal themes. A **universal theme** is a message about life that is true throughout time and in all places. This is true of art masterpieces that continue to speak to people everywhere.

SCIENCE AND TECHNOLOGY

Technology is the use of knowledge, tools, and skills to solve problems. Science is a way of understanding the world through observation and the testing of ideas. Technology is often developed to solve problems posed by the environment we live in. Its use is influenced by factors such as politics, economics, and belief systems. For example, some countries restrict Internet use. Advances in science and technology have made life easier and have changed society. Vaccines have prevented diseases. Electricity and computers have transformed daily life and work for most of the world's people.

> **What are three examples of technology that have changed lives?**
> _____
> _____
> _____

CHALLENGE ACTIVITY

Critical Thinking: Make Inferences Consider all of the parts of your culture that have been influenced by other cultures. During a normal day, keep a list of all the things you use or do that you think have been influenced by other cultures.

DIRECTIONS On the line provided before each statement, write **T** if
a statement is true and **F** if a statement is false. If the statement is
false, write the term that would make the statement correct on the
line after each sentence.

_____ 1. The language you speak and the sports you play are examples of
underline{culture traits}.

_____

_____ 2. underline{Cultural universals} can create an interesting mix of ideas but
sometimes can lead to conflict.

_____

_____ 3. When more than one cultural group lives in an area, this is called a
underline{cultural diffusion}.

_____

_____ 4. A great masterpiece of art, music, or literature has a underline{universal theme}.

_____

_____ 5. Family, education, religion, and government are all examples of basic
underline{ethnic groups}.

_____

_____ 6. A underline{culture region} can be one country or many countries.

_____

cultural diffusion	culture region	culture trait	cultural universal
ethnic group	multicultural society	social institutions	universal theme

DIRECTIONS On a separate sheet of paper, use four of the terms
from the word bank to write a summary of what you learned in the
lesson.

Guided Reading Workbook

The Human World

MAIN IDEAS
1. The study of population patterns helps geographers learn about the world.
2. Population statistics and trends are important measures of population change.

Key Terms and Places

population total number of people in a given area

population density measure of the number of people living in an area, usually expressed as persons per square mile or square kilometer

birthrate annual number of births per 1,000 people

migration process of moving from one place to live in another

Lesson Summary
POPULATION PATTERNS

Population is the total number of people in a given area. Population patterns show how human populations change over time and tell us much about our world.

Population density is a measure of the number of people living in an area, expressed as persons per square mile or square kilometer. The more people per square mile, the more crowded it is and more limited space is. In places with a high density, land is expensive, buildings are taller, and roads are more crowded. However, there are usually more resources and jobs. Places with low density have more space, less traffic, and more open land, but goods and services may be in short supply.

Areas that are less populated are usually difficult to live in. They may be deserts or mountains or have harsh climates that make survival harder. Large clusters of people tend to live in places with good agricultural climates, plenty of vegetation, minerals, and reliable water sources.

> Underline the two sentences that describe the effects of high population density on a place.

> What are conditions like in areas of low population density?
>
> _____
>
> _____

Often, desirable areas attract so many people that there is too much demand for resources. This can change the environment. For example, as regions make room for more people, the amount of available farmland shrinks and local ecosystems are in danger. There is more demand for food and water, which can lead to shortages.

What are three problems caused by population growth?
_____
_____
_____

POPULATION CHANGE

The number of people living in an area affects jobs, housing, schools, medical care, available food, and many other things. Geographers track population changes by studying important statistics, movement of people, and population trends.

Three statistics are important to studying a country's population over time. **Birthrate** is the annual number of births per 1,000 people. Death rate is the annual number of deaths per 1,000 people. The rate of natural increase is the rate at which a population is changing. It is determined by subtracting the death rate from the birthrate.

Underline the sentence that tells how to calculate the rate of natural increase.

A population is shrinking if the death rate is higher than the birthrate. In most countries, the birthrate is higher than the death rate, and those populations are growing. The United States has a low rate of natural increase and is growing slowly. Other countries, like Mali, have a high natural increase that could double its population in 20 years.

High rates can make it hard for countries to develop economically because they need to provide jobs, education, and medical care for a growing population. Many governments track population patterns so they can better address the needs of their citizens.

Why do high rates of natural increase make it hard for a country to develop economically?
_____
_____
_____
_____

Migration is a common cause of population change. It is the process of moving from one place to live in another. People may be pushed to leave a place because of problems there, such as war, famine, drought, or lack of jobs. Other people may be pulled to move to find political or religious freedom or economic opportunities in a new place.

For thousands of years, Earth's population growth was slow and steady. In the last 200 years, it has grown very rapidly due to better health care and improved food production. Currently, many industrialized countries have low rates of natural increase, while countries that are less industrialized often have very high growth. Fast growth can put a strain on resources, jobs, and government aid.

> Why has the world's population grown faster in the last 200 years?
>
> _____
>
> _____
>
> _____

CHALLENGE ACTIVITY

Critical Thinking: Identify Cause and Effect Find out the population density of your city or town. Write down ways that this density affects your life and the lives of others.

DIRECTIONS Read each sentence, and fill in the blank with the word in the word pair that best completes the sentence.

1. The study of human _____ focuses on the total number of people in a given area. (**population/migration**)

2. Studying the _____ is one way to track the percentage of natural increase in the population. (**population density/birthrate**)

3. Calculating _____ can tell us whether a population is growing or shrinking. (**natural increase/population density**)

4. _____ is a common cause of population change. (**Birthrate/Migration**)

5. Land is more expensive in areas with higher _____. (**population density/population patterns**)

birthrate	migration	natural increase
population	population density	population patterns

DIRECTIONS Look up three terms from the word bank in a dictionary. On a separate sheet of paper, write the dictionary definition of the term that is closest to the definition used in your textbook. Then write a sentence using each term correctly.

The Human World

MAIN IDEAS
1. Natural resources and trade routes are important factors in determining location for settlements.
2. Areas can be defined as urban or rural.
3. Spatial patterns describe ways that people build settlements.
4. New technology has improved the interaction of regions with nearby and distant places.

Key Terms and Places

settlement any place where a community is established

trade route path used by people for buying and selling goods

urban related to cities and their surrounding areas

suburb residential community immediately outside of a city

metropolitan area large urban area

megalopolis area where several metropolitan areas grow together

rural related to areas that are found outside of cities

spatial pattern placement of people and objects on Earth and the space between them

linear settlements communities grouped along the length of a resource

cluster settlements communities grouped around or at the center of a resource

grid settlements communities that are laid out according to a network of transportation routes

commerce substantial exchange of goods between cities, states, or countries

Lesson Summary
THE IMPORTANCE OF LOCATION

A **settlement** is any place where a community is started. Settlements can be as small as a remote island village or as large as a very populated city. People often settle near natural resources. Early settlements were near freshwater and good farmland. In the 1800s many cities started as mining centers near coal and iron resources.

> **Where do people often settle?**
> _____

Trade routes are also important to settlements. A **trade route** is a path people use to sell and buy goods. Many settlements started on trade routes, and they grew into important trading centers where major routes met. These centers also were important politically because of their wealth and the different groups that met there.

> **What two factors made some trading centers more important than others?**
>
> _____ _____
>
> _____
>
> _____
>
> _____

URBAN AND RURAL

Geographers classify settlements by certain patterns. **Urban** areas are cities and their surroundings. They are heavily populated and developed, with many buildings and roads. Most urban jobs are not related to the land. Small urban areas might include a city center and a **suburb,** which is a residential area just outside the city. A large urban area, called a **metropolitan area,** might include an entire city, a number of suburbs, and surrounding areas. When several metropolitan areas grow into each other, they form a **megalopolis.** An example of this is the cluster of cities that includes Boston, New York, Philadelphia, Baltimore, and Washington, DC.

> **How is population density different in rural and urban areas?**
>
> _____
>
> _____
>
> _____
>
> _____

Rural areas are found outside of cities. They are usually lightly populated and their economies are tied to the land. Many are built around agriculture, forestry, mining, and recreation.

SPATIAL PATTERNS

Geographers use **spatial patterns** to classify different ways settlements form. They describe how people and objects on Earth are placed in relation to each other. **Linear settlements** are grouped along the length of resource, such as a river. They usually form long, narrow patterns. **Cluster settlements** are grouped around a resource or at its center. For example, many communities are grouped around coal mining operations. **Grid settlements** are laid out along a network of transportation routes. They are

Lesson 3, *continued*

usually in urban areas and may follow a grid made of roads, water routes, or train routes.

> **What type of area is most likely to have a grid settlement?**
>
> _____

REGIONS INTERACT

Commerce is the significant exchange of goods between cities, states, or countries. Urban areas are usually centers of commerce and trade, as well as government. They are often hubs for education, communication, transportation, and innovation. That is why many people live in or near urban areas.

Advances in television, satellites, computers, and the Internet improved communication. This made it easier for cities to create services aimed at nearby regions. It helped them reach markets around the world. Advances in transportation have made the world seem smaller because it is easier to travel great distances in a shorter amount of time.

> **Circle two important advancements that have helped commerce in cities grow.**

CHALLENGE ACTIVITY

Critical Thinking: Identify Cause and Effect

Look into the history of the place where you live and answer the following questions. What was the main source of commerce when your area was first settled? How did that affect where the settlement was first built and its spatial pattern? How has the area changed over the years?

DIRECTIONS Read each sentence and fill in the blank with the
word in the word pair that best completes the sentence.

1. A metropolitan area usually contains a(n) _____ area.
   (**megalopolis/urban**)

2. A rural community is likely to have started as a _____
   near a river. (**linear settlement/suburb**)

cluster settlements	commerce	grid settlement	linear settlement
megalopolis	metropolitan area	rural	settlement
spatial pattern	suburb	trade route	urban

DIRECTIONS On the line provided before each statement, write **T** if
the statement is true and **F** if the statement is false. If the statement
is false, write the term from the word bank that would make the
statement correct on the line after each sentence.

_____ 3. The substantial exchange of goods between cities, states, or countries
is called <u>trade route</u>.

_____

_____ 4. Cluster settlements are an example of a <u>metropolitan area</u>.

_____

_____ 5. A <u>suburb</u> is usually part of an urban area.

_____

_____ 6. Economies of <u>rural</u> areas are often built around agriculture, forestry,
mining, and recreation.

_____

_____ 7. A <u>grid settlement</u> is laid out according to a network of transportation
routes.

_____

The Human World

MAIN IDEAS
1. Geographers examine how environmental conditions shape people's lives.
2. Human activity changes specific places, regions, and the world as a whole.

Key Terms and Places

terraced farming form of farming on steps carved into steep hillsides to create flat land for growing crops

slash-and-burn agriculture form of farming where trees and plants in heavily forested areas are cut down and burned to clear the land for growing crops

center-pivot irrigation system where a center sprinkler waters crops in a circular field

fracking process that uses large amounts of water and chemicals to break up rocks in order to extract gas or oil

Lesson Summary
RESPONDING TO THE ENVIRONMENT

Geographers are interested in how the environment shapes people's lives. They study human systems, like farming, to see how people respond to environmental conditions. Farming is an important example of the way humans respond to their environment. Over time, humans have developed practices that let them grow food in many types of environmental conditions.

Sometimes people have to change the land. For example, in Peru, ancient Inca carved steps into steep hillsides to create flat fields for crops. This is called **terraced farming.** In thickly forested areas, like the Amazon rain forest, some farmers use **slash-and-burn agriculture.** They cut down trees and then burn them so they can clear land to grow crops. And in the U.S., farmers in dry areas create circular fields so they can water them

> **What is an example of a human system?**
> _____

> **What is the practice of carving steps into hillsides called?**
> _____

with a central sprinkler system called **center-pivot irrigation.**

Sometimes the environment cannot be controlled by humans. Natural hazards like fires, tornados, earthquakes, and hurricanes can be deadly and cause a lot of damage. People prepare for them by building shelters, practicing emergency drills, and following strict building codes.

CHANGING THE ENVIRONMENT

People have always changed their environment by building roads, bridges, and dams. They clear land for farming and housing and dig to find natural resources that give them fuel. Many human activities improve people's lives, but they are not always good for the environment. A dam could destroy the ecosystem of a river. Large cities trap heat and make areas drier.

> Circle six examples of ways humans have changed their environment.

Geographers worry about how humans may create environmental problems like pollution, acid rain, land erosion, and global warming. One concern is the ozone layer, which protects Earth from the sun's harmful rays. The use of products with chemicals called chlorofluorocarbons (CFS) started thinning out the ozone layer. Even though most CFS use has been stopped, the ozone layer has not recovered. It may be one of the causes of global warming, severe storms, and rising sea levels.

> Underline the sentence that explains how the ozone layer helps the planet.

Another concern is **fracking.** This process breaks up rock by injecting large amounts of water and chemicals into cracks. Some people support this process because it supplies oil and natural gas for fuel. Others are against fracking because they are worried it will hurt the environment or pollute drinking water.

> Why do some people support fracking?
> _____
> _____

Governments and environmental groups try to create laws to protect the environment and preserve natural resources. Other groups believe

that some practices are important for economic
growth. No matter what the viewpoint,
environmental issues affect everyone on Earth.
That is why many countries are now coming
together to improve the environment around
the globe.

CHALLENGE ACTIVITY

Critical Thinking: Draw Conclusions Write a
paragraph that explains why some people are for
fracking and some are against it. Use these
arguments to come up with your own conclusion
about whether to support or oppose fracking.

DIRECTIONS Write three words or phrases to describe each term.

1. slash-and-burn agriculture _____

_____

2. terraced farming _____

_____

3. center-pivot irrigation _____

4. fracking _____

_____

| center-pivot irrigation | environment | fracking |
| ozone layer | slash-and-burn agriculture | terraced farming |

DIRECTIONS On a separate sheet of paper, use at least three terms
from the word bank to write a short story about what you learned in
the lesson.

Government and Citizenship

MAIN IDEAS
1. The world is divided into physical and human borders.
2. The nations of the world interact through trade and foreign policy.
3. The nations of the world form a world community that resolves conflicts and addresses global issues.

Key Terms and Places

borders a country's political boundaries

sovereign nation government having complete authority over a geographic area

foreign policy a nation's plan for interacting with other countries of the world

diplomacy process of conducting relations between countries

national interest a country's economic, cultural, or military goals

United Nations an organization of the world's countries that promotes peace and security around the globe

human rights rights that all people deserve, such as rights to equality and justice

humanitarian aid assistance to people in distress

Lesson Summary
BOUNDARIES AND BORDERS

Every country has political boundaries, or **borders,** which mark its territory. Within a country, smaller political units such as cities, counties, and states each have their own borders. There are two main types of political boundaries: physical borders and human borders. Physical features such as mountains, deserts, lakes, and oceans make physical borders. These physical features rarely shift. Rivers are also used as boundaries, but the changing course of a river can create border difficulties.

There are two main types of human borders: cultural and geometric. A cultural boundary based on religion was used to divide Muslim Pakistan from mostly Hindu India. Geometric boundaries are borders that do not follow

> **What are the two main types of political boundaries?**
>
> _____

national or cultural patterns. Often, they are straight lines based on lines of latitude or longitude.

NATIONS OF THE WORLD

The establishment of borders is one of the characteristics of a **sovereign nation,** or a government that has complete authority over a geographic area. Sovereign nations rule independently from governments outside their borders. They rule over everyone in their territory and make decisions about domestic, or internal, affairs. They can also defend themselves against foreign invasion.

Sovereign nations interact with other nations through trade and **foreign policy.** Trade allows nations to get the goods they need in exchange for the goods they have or can make. A nation's foreign policy is its plan for interacting with other countries of the world. Foreign policy tools include **diplomacy** and foreign aid. Diplomacy is the process of conducting relations between countries. Diplomacy is used to maintain national security, prevent war, negotiate an end to conflicts, solve problems, and establish communication between countries. Foreign aid is economic or military assistance to another country. Each country shapes its foreign policy to help reach its economic, cultural, or military goals. These make up its **national interest.**

A WORLD COMMUNITY

Nations around the world are connected closely through trade, diplomacy, and foreign aid. What happens in one place affects others. The world community works together to promote cooperation between countries. When conflicts occur, countries from around the world try to settle them. The **United Nations** (UN) is an

> Underline the sentence describing a sovereign nation's authority within its borders.

> List two foreign policy tools.
>
> _____

Lesson 1, *continued*

association of nearly 200 countries dedicated to promoting peace and security. It also works to guarantee **human rights,** or rights that all people deserve. These rights include political rights, social and economic rights, freedom of expression, and equality before the law. The UN sometimes places sanctions, or penalties, on countries, groups, or individuals who have broken international laws.

> **Underline the sentence that describes the main goals of the United Nations.**

Some groups provide humanitarian and development assistance to conflict- and poverty-stricken countries around the world. Humanitarian organizations providing aid in areas of conflict are protected by the Geneva Conventions. The Geneva Conventions are international humanitarian laws that regulate the conduct of armed conflict in all nations. They protect civilians, medics, and aid workers, along with the wounded, sick, and prisoners of war.

> **What are the Geneva Conventions?**
>
> _____
> _____
> _____
> _____
> _____
> _____
> _____

Crises such as earthquakes, floods, droughts, or tsunamis can leave people in great need. Groups from around the world provide **humanitarian aid,** or assistance to people in distress. Some groups aid refugees or provide medical care and vaccinations.

CHALLENGE ACTIVITY
Critical Thinking: Draw Conclusions
Look at a map showing the border between Canada and the United States. Write a description of the border using the following words: physical borders, human borders, and geometric borders.

DIRECTIONS Read each sentence, and fill in the blank with the word in the word pair that best completes the sentence.

1. There are two main types of _____, physical and human. (**borders/humanitarian aid**)

2. A government that rules over everyone in its territory and makes decisions about domestic affairs is a _____. (**sovereign nation/ United Nations**)

3. A nation's plan for interacting with other countries is its _____. (**diplomacy/foreign policy**)

4. A nation's economic, cultural, or military goals make up its _____. (**foreign policy/national interest**)

5. The process of conducting relations between countries is called _____. (**diplomacy/foreign policy**)

6. Freedom of expression and equality before the law are examples of _____. (**diplomacy/human rights**)

borders	diplomacy	foreign policy
human rights	humanitarian aid	national interest
sovereign nation	United Nations	

DIRECTIONS Answer each question by writing a sentence that contains at least two terms from the word bank.

7. What is the purpose of political boundaries?

_____

_____

8. How do sovereign nations interact with one another?

_____

_____

9. How do countries around the world deal with conflict and disaster?

_____

_____

Government and Citizenship

MAIN IDEAS
1. Limited governments of the world include democracies.
2. Unlimited governments of the world include totalitarian governments.
3. Most human rights abuses occur under unlimited governments of the world.

Key Terms and Places

limited government government that has legal limits on its power

constitution written plan of government that outlines its purposes, powers, and limitations

democracy form of government in which the people elect leaders and rule by majority

direct democracy government in which citizens meet in popular assembly to discuss issues and vote for leaders

representative democracy indirect democracy in which citizens vote for representatives who decide on issues and make laws on their behalf

common good welfare of the community

unlimited government government in which power is concentrated in the hands of a single leader or small group

totalitarian government government that controls all aspects of society

Lesson Summary
LIMITED GOVERNMENT

Governments make and enforce laws, regulate business and trade, and provide aid to people. A **limited government** has legal limits on its power, usually in the form of a constitution. A **constitution** is a written plan outlining the government's purposes, powers, and limitations. A **democracy** is a form of limited government in which the people elect leaders and rule by majority. In a **direct democracy,** citizens meet regularly in assembly to discuss issues and vote for leaders.

Most democratic governments today are **representative democracies.** The citizens vote for representatives to decide on issues and make laws

What is a constitution?
_____
_____
_____
_____
_____

on their behalf. Two major forms of
representative democratic governments today are
presidential and parliamentary democracies. In a
presidential democracy, the president is elected
by the people and is directly accountable to them.
Power is shared among three branches of
government. In a parliamentary democracy, the
head of government is directly accountable to the
legislature, or parliament. The legislative branch
also holds executive functions. Most of the
world's democratic governments today are
parliamentary democracies. A few nations are
also constitutional monarchies.

> **Underline the two forms of representative democracies most common today.**

In a limited government, both the government
and individuals must obey the laws. These
governments balance the welfare of the
community, or the **common good,** with individual
welfare. Democracies have social welfare systems
that seek to improve the quality of their citizens'
lives, and they protect their citizens' rights and
freedoms.

> **What two things do limited governments balance?**
> _____
> _____
> _____
> _____

UNLIMITED GOVERNMENTS

In a limited government, everyone, including
leaders, must obey the law. In an **unlimited
government,** there are no limits on a ruler's power.
Power in an authoritarian government is
concentrated in the hands of a single leader or
group. A **totalitarian government** is authoritarian
rule at its most extreme. Totalitarian governments
exercise control over all aspects of society—the
government, economy, and even people's beliefs
and actions. In these societies, citizens have no
way to change the government. Examples of
totalitarian governments include China under
Mao Zedong and North Korea under Kim
Jong-un.

> **List two examples of totalitarian governments.**
> _____
> _____
> _____

In unlimited governments, the rights of citizens
are rarely recognized or protected, and citizens
may not be able to take part in government or

openly express their views. Rulers often use force to put down opposition movements. They ignore or change constitutions or laws intended to restrict their power.

Shortly after World War II, the Chinese government created an authoritarian Communist system, imprisoning or killing those who spoke out against its policies. Although plans for industrial development were instituted, widespread food shortages led to the deaths of tens of millions by the early 1960s.

A gradual retreat from many of these early policies began in the late 1970s, but there were limits to what officials would allow. In 1989 the government violently crushed a peaceful pro-democracy student demonstration in China's capital, Beijing. This became known as the Tiananmen Square Massacre.

China's government today is balancing authoritarian rule, economic growth, and slow political reform.

> **What was the name given to the 1989 pro-democracy demonstration in Beijing?**
> _____
> _____

HUMAN RIGHTS ABUSES

People today believe that everyone has human rights, or rights that all people deserve. These rights include equality, justice, political rights, and social and economic rights. Human rights abuses are most common in countries that are not free or are only partially free. These abuses include torture, slavery, and murder. Abuses in democratic countries often occur as a result of inaction.

The United Nations (UN) is an international organization committed to guaranteeing human rights for all people. The United States recognizes that respect for human rights promotes peace and deters aggression.

> **What are some examples of human rights abuses?**
> _____
> _____

CHALLENGE ACTIVITY

Critical Thinking: Compare and Contrast Write a
paragraph that compares and contrasts limited
and unlimited governments.

common good	constitution	democracy
direct democracy	unlimited government	representative democracy
totalitarian government		

DIRECTIONS On the line provided before each statement, write **T** if
a statement is true and **F** if a statement is false. If the statement is
false, write a term from the word bank that would make the
statement correct on the line after each sentence.

_____ 1. Korea under Kim Jong-un is an example of a <u>direct democracy</u>.

_____

_____ 2. <u>Democracy</u> is a form of government in which one person or a few
people hold power.

_____

_____ 3. A government in which the state has control over all aspects of society
is called a <u>totalitarian government</u>.

_____

_____ 4. In <u>unlimited governments,</u> people elect leaders and rule by majorities.

_____

_____ 5. A <u>constitution</u> enforces the legal limits of a government's power.

_____

_____ 6. A constitutional monarchy is an example of a <u>totalitarian government</u>.

_____

_____ 7. The welfare of a whole community is known as the <u>common good</u>.

_____

Guided Reading Workbook

Government and Citizenship

Lesson 3

MAIN IDEAS
1. The duties and roles of citizenship help to make representative government work.
2. Good citizens accept their responsibilities for maintaining a strong democracy.
3. Citizens influence government through public opinion.
4. The type of government in some societies influences the roles of the citizens in those societies.

Key Terms and Places

representative government system in which people are the ultimate source of government authority

draft law that requires men of certain ages and qualifications to join the military

jury duty required service of citizens to act as a member of a jury

political party group of citizens with similar views on public issues who work to put their ideas into effective government action

interest groups organizations of people with a common interest that try to influence government policies and decisions

public opinion the way large groups of citizens think about issues and people

nonrepresentative government a government in which government power is unlimited and citizens have few, if any, rights

Lesson Summary
DUTIES AND ROLES OF CITIZENSHIP

In the United States, citizens are the ultimate source of government authority. This is called a **representative government.** For this type of government to work, citizens must perform certain duties. One duty of citizens is to obey the law. A democracy needs educated citizens to choose leaders and understand issues. In the United States, you must attend school until the age of 16.

Who is the source of government authority in a representative government?
_____

Lesson 3, *continued*

Citizens must pay taxes. Taxes fund public services such as road repair, police protection, and national security. When the country needs people to fight wars, it may issue a **draft.** A draft requires men of certain ages and qualifications to serve in the military. Citizens must also serve on a jury if they are called to do so. This service is called **jury duty.** The Constitution guarantees citizens the right to a trial by their peers—their fellow citizens.

> Underline the three responsibilities of citizens.

RIGHTS AND RESPONSIBILITIES

In a representative government, citizens also have responsibilities—tasks they should do as citizens but that are not required by law.

In order to give consent to our lawmakers in government, we should vote. Voting is a way to show our decision makers whether we agree with their opinions on issues. Becoming informed about key issues, candidates, and current events will help you make informed choices when you vote. You might also take part in government by joining a **political party.** Political parties nominate or select candidates to run for political office.

Citizens can also join an **interest group.** These are organizations made up of people sharing a common goal. Interest groups try to influence government policies and decisions.

Another way to help society is by volunteering in your community. By knowing your own rights as a citizen, you can make sure you respect the rights of the people around you. You should also know if someone else's rights are being violated.

> What are some of our responsibilities as citizens?
>
> _____
> _____
> _____
> _____
> _____
> _____
> _____

CITIZENS AND THE MEDIA

The media plays an important role in free societies such as the United States. Newspapers, magazines, radio, television, film, the Internet, and books help to keep people informed. What citizens learn from the media shapes

> Underline the influences that affect public opinion.

Lesson 3, *continued*

public opinion, or the way large groups of citizens think about issues and people. Public opinion on any particular issue may be very diverse.

Opinions are also influenced by family, friends, teachers, and clubs. Citizens rely on mass media to help them decide how to vote on important issues or candidates. However, effective citizenship requires critical thinking about what you see, hear, and read.

CITIZENSHIP IN OTHER SOCIETIES

Other representative governments may have similar roles and responsibilities for their citizens. These may not be the same as those of U.S. citizens. **Nonrepresentative governments** are governments in which citizens have few, if any, rights. The government maintains all the power. At times, citizens become so dissatisfied that they revolt against their leaders.

> **What rights do citizens have under nonrepresentative governments?**
>
> _____
> _____
> _____
> _____

CHALLENGE ACTIVITY

Critical Thinking: Explain Explain why representative government requires the involvement of the country's citizens.

draft	interest group	jury duty	nonrepresentative government
political party	public opinion	representative government	

DIRECTIONS Answer each question by writing a sentence that contains at least one term from the word bank.

1. How does a representative government work?

_____

_____

2. When might the United States issue a draft?

_____

_____

3. Name some duties and responsibilities of a United States citizen.

_____

_____

4. What is a nonrepresentative government?

_____

_____

5. Explain how the Constitution guarantees citizens a right to a trial by their peers.

_____

_____

6. How are candidates for political office usually chosen?

_____

_____

7. How can citizens in the United States influence the government?

_____

_____

Economics

MAIN IDEAS
1. The main problem in economics is scarcity.
2. Scarcity shapes how societies use factors of production.

Key Terms and Places

economy system of producing, selling, and buying goods and services

scarcity problem of having unlimited human wants in a world of limited resources

opportunity cost value of the thing given up when a choice is made

profit money an individual or business has left after paying expenses

factors of production basic economic resources needed to produce goods and services

contraction problem that can occur when a factor of production is in short supply

expansion benefit that can happen when a factor of production is increased

economic interdependence system in which one nation depends on another to provide goods and services it does not produce

Lesson Summary
KEY CONCEPTS

An **economy** is a system of producing, selling, and buying goods and services. There are global, national, and local economies. Goods are products that people buy and use such as clothes, furniture, and toothpaste. Services are actions that people provide such as styling hair, repairing cars, or mowing lawns. Consumers are the people who buy goods or services for personal use. The study of economies is called economics.

All economies face the same basic problem, called **scarcity.** People's wants are unlimited, but the resources available to satisfy their wants are limited. This leads to scarcity.

> How are goods different from services?
> _____
> _____
> _____
> _____

Scarcity causes people to make choices, or tradeoffs, between things they need and things they want. Since every choice to buy something is a choice not to buy something else, every choice has an **opportunity cost.** This is the value of the thing given up in any choice or tradeoff. These choices by consumers help determine what sellers will produce and what they will charge for it. *Supply* is the amount of a good and service that businesses produce. *Demand* is the desire to have a good or service and the ability to pay for it. Supply and demand generally determine the price of a good or service. Businesses will produce more goods or services when they can charge a high price for it. Consumers prefer to buy more goods or services when the price is low. If the prices of goods or services rise, consumers will buy less.

Incentives, or benefits, influence economic choices. **Profit** is a major incentive for individuals and businesses. Profit is the money left after paying expenses. The desire to make money, or the profit incentive, leads many people to start a business. Consumer incentives include saving money and receiving something extra with a purchase.

SCARCITY AND RESOURCE USE

There are three basic questions that must be answered when producing goods and services: What will be produced? How will it be produced? For whom will it be produced? Economists study **factors of production** to understand how societies answer these questions. There are four main factors of production: *natural resources, capital, labor,* and *entrepreneurs.* There is a limited supply of each factor. If a factor of production is in short supply, the situation could cause a **contraction** of the business. On the other hand, if

> What two factors generally determine the price of a good or service?
>
> _____

> Underline three economic incentives.

> Circle the three basic questions for producing goods and services.

a factor of production is increased, then the benefit is known as an **expansion** of the business.

Natural resources include raw materials to produce goods and land on which a business is built. Service companies need to be located near their potential customers. Capital, or capital goods, is the total of all the equipment or property. Financial capital is the money a business uses to buy the capital goods needed for production. Labor is human time, effort, skills, and talent needed to produce goods and services. Entrepreneurs are the people who come up with ideas for new products or businesses. They risk their labor and capital in hopes of making a profit. Availability or lack of each factor of production can cause contraction or expansion of a business.

The factors of production are not distributed equally. This causes countries to decide what to produce based on their resources. This can lead to specialization, when individuals or businesses focus on a narrow range of products. The availability of resources also shapes how a society produces goods and services.

Scarcity of resources can lead to trade between nations and to **economic interdependence.** A country that needs to trade with another country to get a key resource becomes dependent on that trade.

> **What are the two kinds of capital?**
>
> _____
>
> _____

> **Underline three ways a nation's economy is shaped by the unequal distribution of factors of production.**

CHALLENGE ACTIVITY

Critical Thinking: Draw Conclusions

This week, make a list of everything you purchase. Determine how many purchases were for goods and how many were for services. Did you have to make a choice to buy one item over another? If so, list the opportunity costs of the item you decided not to buy. Evaluate your spending habits at the end of the week.

DIRECTIONS Read each sentence, and fill in the blank with the word in the word pair that best completes the sentence.

1. The value of something given up in a choice or tradeoff is called the

   _____. (**factors of production/opportunity cost**)

2. Unlimited human wants create _____ in the world because of limited resources. (**profit/scarcity**)

3. A nation's _____ is its system of producing, selling, and buying goods and services. (**economy/scarcity**)

4. The money an individual or business has left after paying expenses is called

   _____. (**capital/profit**)

5. Nations that rely on trade with one another for supplies of scarce resources

   experience _____. (**economic interdependence/scarcity**)

6. When a factor of production is increased, the result can be a(n)

   _____ of the business. (**contraction/expansion**)

capital	contraction
economic interdependence	economy
expansion	factors of production
opportunity cost	profit
scarcity	

DIRECTIONS On a separate sheet of paper, answer each question by writing a sentence that contains at least one term from the word bank.

7. What happens when you want to go to a movie and buy music but you only have enough money for one thing or the other?

8. How can an economic incentive lead a person to start a business?

9. How do natural resources, labor, capital, and entrepreneurs relate to one another?

Economics

> **MAIN IDEAS**
> 1. There are three basic types of economic systems.
> 2. Contemporary societies have mixed economies.
> 3. The United States benefits from a free enterprise system.
> 4. Governments provide public goods.
> 5. Geographers categorize countries based on levels of economic development and range of economic activities.

Key Terms and Places

traditional economy people's work is based on long-established customs

command economy government controls the economy

market economy economy based on private ownership, free trade, and competition

mixed economy combination of traditional, market, and command economic systems

free enterprise system economic system in which few limits are placed on business activities

public goods goods and services provided by the government for public consumption

agricultural industries businesses that focus on growing crops and raising livestock

manufacturing industries businesses that make finished products from raw materials

wholesale industries businesses that sell to other businesses

retail industries businesses that sell directly to consumers

service industries businesses that provide services rather than goods

developed countries countries with strong economies and a high quality of life

developing countries countries with weak economies and a lower quality of life

gross domestic product (GDP) value of all goods and services produced within a country in a single year

Lesson Summary
MAIN TYPES OF ECONOMIC SYSTEMS

An economic system is the way in which a society organizes the production and distribution of goods and services. A **traditional economy** is based on long-established customs of who does what work. A **command economy** is controlled by

> Underline the three types of economic systems.

Lesson 2, *continued*

the government. A **market economy** is based on private ownership, free trade, and competition.

MODERN ECONOMIES

Most countries have one of three types of **mixed economies:** communist, capitalist, and socialist. In a communist society, the government owns all factors of production. In a capitalist economy, individuals and businesses own the factors of production. In socialist economies, the government controls some of the basic factors of production.

> **What are the three types of mixed economies?**
> _____
> _____

THE FREE ENTERPRISE SYSTEM

U.S. capitalism is sometimes called the **free enterprise system.** Individuals are free to exchange goods and services and to own and operate businesses with little government intervention. The ability to make a profit is one of the key advantages of this system. To function properly, the free enterprise system requires that people obey laws, be truthful, and avoid behaviors that harm others.

> **What is a free enterprise system?**
> _____
> _____
> _____
> _____
> _____
> _____

GOVERNMENT AND PUBLIC GOODS

Governments today provide expensive or important services to large groups of people who might otherwise have to do without the service. These government goods and services are called **public goods.** They include schools, highways, and police and fire protection. Public goods are paid for through taxes. Because scarcity affects government, too, a government must determine the opportunity cost of public goods.

> **How are public goods paid?**
> _____

Governments also use regulations, or rules, to control business behavior. These rules must be helpful and fair. The most common government regulations include protection for public health and safety and for the environment.

ECONOMIC ACTIVITIES AND DEVELOPMENT

There are three levels of economic activity, or areas in which people make a living. People in primary industries harvest products from the earth. An example is **agricultural industries,** in which people focus on growing crops and raising livestock. In secondary industries, the natural resources and raw materials are made into products. **Manufacturing industries** are secondary industries. In tertiary industries, people provide goods and services to customers. **Wholesale industries, retail industries,** and **service industries** are tertiary industries. Health care workers, mechanics, and teachers work in service industries.

> Circle three types of industries that are tertiary industries.

The world's most powerful nations are **developed countries,** countries with strong economies and a high quality of life. **Developing countries** have less productive economies and a lower quality of life. One indicator, or measure, of a country's wealth is **gross domestic product (GDP).** GDP is the value of all goods and services produced within a country in a single year. Literacy, life expectancy, and overall level of industrialization are other indicators of a country's wealth.

> Underline the four indicators of a country's wealth.

CHALLENGE ACTIVITY

Critical Thinking: Compare and Contrast How is the American free enterprise system different from communist and socialist economies? Write a paragraph explaining the differences.

DIRECTIONS Read each sentence, and fill in the blank with the word in the word pair that best completes the sentence.

1. Businesses known as _____ make finished products from raw materials. (**manufacturing industries/retail industries**)

2. In a _____, few limits are placed on business activities. (**command economy/free enterprise system**)

3. _____ industries focus on growing crops and raising livestock. (**Agricultural/Wholesale**)

4. Countries with less productive economies and a lower quality of life are known as _____. (**developing countries/developed countries**)

5. Police and fire protection are examples of _____. (**public goods/gross domestic product**)

agricultural industries	command economy
developed countries	developing countries
free enterprise system	gross domestic product
manufacturing industries	market economy
mixed economy	public goods
retail industries	service industries
traditional economy	wholesale industries

DIRECTIONS Look up three terms from the word bank in an encyclopedia or dictionary. On a separate sheet of paper, write the encyclopedia or dictionary definition of the term that is closest to the definition used in your textbook. Then write a sentence using each term correctly.

Economics

MAIN IDEAS
1. Money is used as a medium of exchange, a store of value, and a unit of account.
2. Banks are places to store money, earn money, and borrow money.
3. People can use their earnings to build wealth.

Key Terms and Places

barter trade a good or service for a good or service provided by someone else

money anything that people will accept as payment for goods and services

medium of exchange means through which goods and services can be exchanged

store of value something that holds its value over time

unit of account yardstick of economic value in exchanges

interest rate percentage of the total amount of money loaned or borrowed

assets things of economic value that a person or company owns

income money paid to a person or business for goods or services

savings income not spent on immediate wants

investment use of money today in a way that earns future benefits

Lesson Summary
PURPOSES OF MONEY

Without money, people must **barter,** or trade, for goods and services they want or need. Barter works when both people want to exchange particular goods or services at the same time. If only one wants to exchange, barter does not work. This difficulty led to the invention of money. **Money** is anything that people will accept as payment for goods and services. Today it is generally metal coins or paper currency, but other items have been used as money.

Money performs three functions. First, it serves as a **medium of exchange,** or means through which goods and services can be exchanged. Second, it serves as a **store of value,** something that holds its value over time. This

> Why is money easier to use than barter?
>
> _____
> _____
> _____
> _____
> _____
> _____
> _____

> Underline the three functions of money.

allows money to be saved for use in the future.
Third, money serves as a **unit of account.** It
allows people to measure the relative costs of
goods and services. In the United States, the
economic value of all goods and services can be
measured by the dollar, the nation's basic
monetary unit.

BANKS AND THE ECONOMY

Banks are like money stores, where people buy
(borrow) money and sell (lend) it. Customers
store money, earn money, and borrow money at
a bank. Banks are businesses, so they earn
money by charging interest or fees for these
services.

> **How do banks earn money?**
> _____
> _____
> _____
> _____

Banks have three main functions. First, they
are safe places where people can store money.
Second, customers can earn money when they
store their savings in banks. Savings accounts and
some checking accounts offer a payment, called
interest. The bank is borrowing the money from
the customer, and the customer is paid for the use
of the money. Third, banks loan this money to
other customers who want to borrow money for a
purchase. These borrowers pay the bank interest
for the use of the money. The amount of interest
paid is based on an **interest rate.** When interest
rates are high, people are more likely to save their
money. When interest rates are low, they may
borrow or shift their savings to investments with
higher interest rates.

> **Underline the three main functions of banks.**

MONEY MANAGEMENT

People and businesses save and invest money in
order to increase their financial resources.
Savings and investments are good ways to gain
assets, which are things a person or business
owns that have economic value.

Every person who has a job that pays a wage
earns **income.** Businesses also earn income by

selling goods and services. People can do two things with their income: spend it or save it. **Savings** is income not spent on immediate wants. Common options for saving money include savings accounts, certificates of deposit (CDs), and stocks. Money in a savings account can be used at any time, but the interest rate is low. CDs pay a higher interest rate, but the money is deposited for a set amount of time, so it is not easily available.

What two things can people do with their income?
_____

Investment in stock gives a person partial ownership in a company. If the stock price increases, the stock owner makes money. If the stock price drops, the stock owner can lose money. People decide whether to save or invest their money by choosing an investment goal. Generally, investments that carry a higher risk of losing some or all of the money are more likely to earn high rewards. Lower-risk investments such as savings accounts and CDs earn lower rewards. Inflation is another risk that savers must consider. Inflation affects the purchasing power of money, so the money saved may not buy as much in the future as it does in the present.

What happens to a stock owner if the stock price increases?
_____
_____
_____

CHALLENGE ACTIVITY

Critical Thinking: Make Inferences Banks charge a higher interest rate for loans than they pay for savings accounts. Why are the interest rates not the same for borrowing and lending?

Name _____ Class _____ Date _____

Lesson 3, *continued*

DIRECTIONS Read each sentence, and fill in the blank with the word in the word pair that best completes the sentence.

1. Money serves as a _____ because it holds its value over time. **(medium of exchange/store of value)**

2. _____ is something that people accept as payment for goods or services. **(Barter/Money)**

3. People saving for retirement want to make wise investments so their _____ will grow and they can live comfortably. **(assets/income)**

4. Stocks are _____ that help people increase their assets. **(units of account/investments)**

5. _____ is the function of money that allows people to measure the relative costs of goods and services. **(Medium of exchange/Unit of account)**

assets	barter
income	interest rate
investment	medium of exchange
money	savings
store of value	unit of account

DIRECTIONS Answer each question by writing a sentence that contains at least one term from the word bank.

6. Which of the three functions of money is the most important, and why?

_____

_____

_____

7. What does a bank do with money it stores?

_____

_____

8. Why might a person invest in CDs rather than savings?

_____

Economics

Lesson 4

MAIN IDEAS
1. Globalization links the world's countries together through culture and trade.
2. Multinational corporations make global trade easier and allow countries to become more interdependent.
3. The world community works together to solve global conflicts and crises.

Key Terms and Places

globalization process in which countries are increasingly linked to each other through culture and trade

popular culture culture traits that are well known and widely accepted

trade barriers any law that limits free trade between nations

free trade trade without trade barriers between nations

Lesson Summary
GLOBALIZATION

People around the world are more closely linked than ever before. **Globalization** is the process in which countries are increasingly linked to each other through culture and trade. Improvements in transportation and communication have increased globalization.

Popular culture refers to culture traits that are well known and widely accepted. These traits can include food, sports, music, and movies. The United States has a great influence on popular culture through American products, television, and the English language. English has become the major global language. It is used for international music, business, science, and education around the world. The United States is, in turn, greatly influenced by other countries. Martial arts movies from Asia are quite popular in the United States, and many foreign words such as *sushi* and *croissant* have become common in the English language.

> Underline the sentence that describes two ways countries are linked together.

> What are four traits that can be considered part of popular culture?
>
> _____
>
> _____
>
> _____

Lesson 4, *continued*

GLOBAL TRADE

Globalization also connects businesses and affects trade. Global trade takes place at a much faster pace than ever because of faster transportation and communication technologies. Telecommunication, computers, and the Internet have made global trade quick and easy.

The expansion of global trade has increased interdependence among the world's countries. Interdependence is a relationship between countries in which they rely on one another for resources, goods, or services. Companies that operate in a number of different countries are called multinational corporations. For their manufacturing plants, these companies select locations where raw materials or labor is cheapest. They often produce different parts of their products on different continents. Many developing nations want multinational corporations to invest in them because they create jobs.

GLOBAL ECONOMIC ISSUES

Countries trade with each other to obtain resources, goods, and services. Developing nations still struggle to gain economic stability because they lack the necessary technologies, well-trained workers, and money for investments. Developed nations provide aid to developing nations through the work of international organizations. The World Bank provides loans for large projects, health care, education, or infrastructure such as roads or power plants. The International Monetary Fund (IMF) offers emergency loans to countries in financial trouble.

Sometimes, governments pass laws to protect their countries' jobs and industries. **Trade barriers** such as quotas, tariffs, and embargoes limit **free trade** between nations. Quotas limit the number of lower-priced products that can be imported. A tariff, or tax on imported goods, protects the

> What four improvements have made global trade faster and easier?
>
> _____
>
> _____
>
> _____

> Why do many developing nations want multinational corporations to invest in them?
>
> _____
>
> _____
>
> _____

> What are two international organizations that aid developing nations?
>
> _____
>
> _____
>
> _____

Lesson 4, *continued*

price of domestic goods. An embargo is a law that cuts off most or all trade with a specific country. Many countries, however, encourage free trade. The World Trade Organization (WTO) has worked with other nations to help trade among nations flow as smoothly and freely as possible.

> **What are three types of trade barriers?**
>
> _____
>
> _____

CHALLENGE ACTIVITY

Critical Thinking: Make Inferences Why do developed nations provide aid to developing nations?

DIRECTIONS Read each sentence, and fill in the blank with the word in the word pair that best completes the sentence.

1. Tariffs, quotas, and embargoes are examples of _____. **(interdependence/trade barriers)**

2. _____ occurs when countries depend on each other for resources, goods, or services. **(Telecommunications/Interdependence)**

3. The _____ provides loans to developing nations so they can build such things as power plants and roads. **(World Bank/World Trade Organization)**

DIRECTIONS On the line provided before each statement, write **T** if the statement is true and **F** if the statement is false. If the statement is false, write the term that would make the statement correct on the line after each sentence.

_____ 4. The process in which countries are linked to one another through culture and trade is called <u>popular culture</u>.

_____

_____ 5. Culture traits such as food, music, movies, and sports are examples of <u>globalization</u>.

_____

_____ 6. As a result of globalization, there is more <u>interdependence</u> among countries.

_____

_____ 7. The World Trade Organization works to create <u>trade barriers</u> between nations.

_____

The United States

MAIN IDEAS
1. Major physical features of the United States include mountains, rivers, and plains.
2. The climate of the United States is wetter in the East and South and drier in the West.
3. The United States is rich in natural resources such as farmland, oil, forests, and minerals.

Key Terms and Places

Appalachian Mountains main mountain range in the East

Great Lakes largest group of freshwater lakes in the world

Mississippi River North America's largest and most important river

tributary smaller stream or river that flows into a larger stream or river

Rocky Mountains enormous mountain range in the West

continental divide area of high ground that divides the flow of rivers toward opposite ends of a continent

Lesson Summary
PHYSICAL FEATURES

The United States is one of the largest countries in the world. On the eastern coast of the United States, the land is flat and close to sea level. This area is called the Atlantic Coastal Plain. Moving west, the land rises to a region called the Piedmont. The land rises higher in the **Appalachian Mountains,** the main mountain range in the East. The highest peak in the Appalachians is about 6,700 feet (2,042 m).

West of the Appalachian Mountains are the Interior Plains. The plains are filled with rolling hills, lakes, and rivers. The main physical features of the Interior Plains are the **Great Lakes.** The Great Lakes are the largest freshwater lake system in the world. They are also an important waterway for trade between the United States and Canada.

> **Where is the Atlantic Coastal Plain?**
>
> _____
>
> _____

> **What is special about the Great Lakes?**
>
> _____
>
> _____
>
> _____

The **Mississippi River** lies west of the Great Lakes. It is the largest and most important river in North America. **Tributaries** of the Mississippi River deposit rich silt that produces fertile farmlands. These farmlands cover most of the Interior Plains.

West of the Mississippi River lie the Great Plains. These are vast areas of grasslands. Further west, the land begins to rise, eventually leading to the **Rocky Mountains.** Many of these mountains reach higher than 14,000 feet (4,267 m). Along the crest of the Rocky Mountains is a ridge that divides North America's rivers. This is called a **continental divide.** Rivers east of the divide mostly flow eastward, and most rivers west of the divide flow westward.

Farther west, mountain ranges include the Cascade Range and the Sierra Nevada. Mountains also stretch north along the Pacific coast. Alaska's Denali, which used to be called Mount McKinley, is the highest mountain in North America.

CLIMATE

The eastern United States is divided into three climate regions. The Northeast has a humid continental climate. To the south, the climate is humid subtropical. Farthest south, most of Florida is warm all year.

The climate in the Interior Plains varies. It is hot and dry in the Great Plains. But in most of the Midwest, the climate is humid continental. In the West, climates are mostly dry. Alaska has subarctic and tundra climates, while Hawaii is tropical.

NATURAL RESOURCES

Our lives are affected by natural resources every day. Much of our paper, food, gas, and electricity come from natural resources in the United States.

What is special about the Mississippi River?
_____
_____
_____

About how high are the highest mountains in the Rocky Mountains?
_____
_____

What is the highest mountain in North America?
_____
_____

Circle the names of the climate regions in the eastern United States.

List four products that come from natural resources found in the United States.
_____
_____

CHALLENGE ACTIVITY

Critical Thinking: Draw Inferences Write three paragraphs describing what makes the physical geography of the United States so diverse.

DIRECTIONS Read each sentence and fill in the blank with the word in the word pair that best completes the sentence.

1. Grasslands cover most of the _____, making the region a good place to grow wheat and other grains. **(Rocky Mountains/Great Plains)**

2. The Missouri and Ohio Rivers are two major tributaries of the _____. **(Great Lakes/Mississippi River)**

3. The _____ separates the flow of North America's rivers, sending some water east into the Mississippi River and some water west into the Pacific Ocean. **(tributary/continental divide)**

Appalachian Mountains	continental divide	Great Lakes
Great Plains	Mississippi River	Rocky Mountains
tributary		

DIRECTIONS On the line provided before each statement, write **T** if a statement is true and **F** if a statement is false. If the statement is false, write the term from the word bank that would make the statement correct on the line after each sentence.

_____ 4. The <u>Rocky Mountains</u> are the main mountain range in the East.

_____

_____ 5. The <u>Mississippi River</u> is (are) an important waterway for trade between the United States and Canada.

_____

DIRECTIONS Write three words or phrases that describe the term.

6. tributary _____

_____

Name _____ Class _____ Date _____

The United States

 MAIN IDEAS

1. The United States, the world's first modern democracy, expanded from the Atlantic coast to the Pacific coast over time.

2. In the United States, different levels of government have different roles, but all levels require the participation of the citizens.

3. The people and culture of the United States are very diverse.

Key Terms and Places

colony territory inhabited and controlled by people from a foreign land

Boston major seaport in the British colonies during the mid-1700s

New York major seaport in the British colonies during the mid-1700s

plantation large farm that grows mainly one crop

pioneers first settlers in the West

U.S. Constitution document spelling out the powers and function of the branches of the federal government

legislative branch responsible for making laws

executive branch carries out and enforces laws

judicial branch interprets the laws in court cases

bilingual people who speak two languages

Lesson Summary
FIRST MODERN DEMOCRACY

Europeans began settling in North America in the 1500s and setting up **colonies.** New cities such as **Boston** and **New York** became major seaports in the British colonies. Thousands of enslaved Africans were brought to the colonies and forced to work on **plantations.**

In the 1770s many British colonists were unhappy with British rule. As a result, colonial representatives adopted the Declaration of Independence in July 1776. To win independence, colonists fought the British in the Revolutionary War. The British were defeated in 1781 at the Battle of Yorktown in Virginia.

> **Name two major seaports in the British colonies.**
> _____
> _____

> **What happened in July 1776?**
> _____
> _____
> _____
> _____

Guided Reading Workbook

After the war, the United States began to
expand west. The first settlers in the West were
called **pioneers.** Many sought land, others were
looking for gold. By 1850 the country stretched
all the way to the Pacific Ocean. The United
States faced two world wars during the 1900s.
After World War II, the United States and the
Soviet Union became rivals in the Cold War,
which lasted until the 1990s.

> **By 1850 the United States stretched from the Atlantic coast to which ocean?**
> _____

GOVERNMENT AND CITIZENSHIP

The United States is a representative democracy.
It is a limited government based on the **U.S.
Constitution.** The Bill of Rights, a part of the
Constitution, protects individual rights such as
the freedoms of speech, press, and religion and
the right to a fair trial.

> **Underline four individual rights protected by the Constitution.**

The federal government has three branches.
Congress, the **legislative branch,** makes laws. The
executive branch, which includes the president
and vice-president, enforces the laws. The **judicial
branch** interprets the laws in court cases. Each
state has its own constitution and government.
Counties and cities have their own local
governments. All levels of government require
the participation of the citizens. Participation
includes voting, paying taxes, and jury service.

> **What are the three branches of the federal government?**
> _____
> _____
> _____

PEOPLE AND CULTURE

Many Americans are descendants of European
immigrants. The United States is also home to
people of many different cultures and ethnic
groups. The United States is a diverse nation,
where many languages are spoken, different
religions are practiced, and a variety of foods are
eaten.

For thousands of years, Native Americans
were the only people living in the Americas.
Descendants of enslaved Africans live
throughout the country, with the highest

population of African Americans living in the South. Asian Americans are descendants of people who came from Asian countries. Many Hispanic Americans originally migrated to the United States from Mexico, Cuba, and other Latin American countries.

When people migrate to the United States, they bring parts of their culture with them, including their religions, food, and music. Some Americans are **bilingual.** Other than English, Spanish is the most widely spoken language in the United States. People of different ethnic groups make the United States a very diverse country.

> Underline the sentence that explains where many Hispanic Americans originally migrated.

> What parts of their culture do people bring with them when they migrate to the United States?
> _____

CHALLENGE ACTIVITY
Critical Thinking: Draw Inferences
Imagine that you are about to turn 18. Make a list of ways you, as a U.S. citizen, can participate in the state, local, and federal government.

DIRECTIONS Look at the set of three terms following each number. On the line provided, write the letter of the term that does not relate to the others.

_____ 1. a. cotton   b. plantation   c. bilingual

_____ 2. a. seaport   b. pioneers   c. New York

_____ 3. a. legislative branch   b. West   c. pioneers

_____ 4. a. Boston   b. judicial branch   c. New York

_____ 5. a. U.S. Constitution   b. Boston   c. executive branch

bilingual	Boston	colony	executive branch
judicial branch	legislative branch	New York	pioneers
plantation	U.S. Constitution		

DIRECTIONS Answer each question by writing a sentence that contains at least one term from the word bank.

_____ 6. What is one reason that the population of the United States is so culturally diverse today?

_____

_____ 7. What was America like before the Revolutionary War?

_____

_____

_____

_____ 8. What makes the government of the United States a limited democracy?

_____

_____

Name _____ Class _____ Date _____

The United States

MAIN IDEAS
1. The United States has four regions—the Northeast, the South, the Midwest, and the West.
2. The United States has a strong economy and a powerful military but is facing the challenge of world terrorism.

Key Terms and Places

Washington, DC the United States capital

Chicago one of the busiest shipping ports on the Great Lakes

Detroit located in Michigan and is the nation's leading automobile producer

Seattle Washington's largest city and home to technology and aerospace companies

terrorism violent attacks to intimidate or cause fear

Lesson Summary
REGIONS OF THE UNITED STATES

Geographers often divide the United States into four main regions. These are the Northeast, the South, the Midwest, and the West.

The Northeast is the smallest region in the United States, as well as the most densely populated. Natural resources in the Northeast include rich farmland, coal, and fishing. Major seaports make it possible to ship products to markets around the world.

The Northeast is covered by a string of large cities called a megalopolis. It stretches from Boston to **Washington, DC.** Other major cities are New York, Philadelphia, and Baltimore.

The South includes coastlines along the Atlantic Ocean and the Gulf of Mexico. The coastal plains provide farmers with rich soils for growing cotton, tobacco, and citrus fruits.

Technology, education, and oil are also important industries in the South. Warm weather and beautiful beaches make tourism an important part of the South's economy.

> **What are the four main regions of the United States?**
> _____
> _____

> **List five cities that make up the megalopolis in the Northeast.**
> _____
> _____
> _____
> _____

> **Underline the sentences that describe the industries that contribute to the South's economy.**

Guided Reading Workbook

The Midwest is one of the world's most productive farming regions. Rich soils deposited by the region's rivers are perfect for raising livestock and producing corn, dairy products, and soybeans.

Most of the major cities in the Midwest, such as **Chicago** and **Detroit,** are located on rivers or the Great Lakes. This makes it easier to transport farm products, coal, and iron ore.

> **Where are the major cities of the Midwest located?**
> _____
> _____

The West is the largest region. California's mild climate and wealth of resources make it home to more than 10 percent of the country's population.

> **What is the largest region in the United States?**
> _____

Ranching, farming, coal, oil, gold, silver, copper, forestry, and fishing are important industries in the West. **Seattle,** Washington's largest city, is home to many industries, including technology and aerospace.

CHANGES IN THE NATION

The United States has faced many challenges in recent years. Trade, technology, and an abundance of natural resources have helped make the U.S. economy strong. However, by the end of 2007, the United States faced a recession, or a sharp decrease in economic activity. The housing market collapsed, some banks and businesses failed, and millions of jobs were lost.

Terrorism continued to threaten the nation's safety. After the deadliest terrorist attack in U.S. history on September 11, 2001, the United States and other world leaders began working together to combat terrorism.

> **What are two major issues the United States has faced in recent years?**
> _____
> _____

In 2008 Barack Obama became the nation's first African American president. In 2016 Donald Trump, a businessman, defeated the Democratic candidate, Hillary Clinton.

CHALLENGE ACTIVITY

Critical Thinking: Explain Think about the physical features, climates, natural resources, industries, and economies of the regions in the United States. Choose the region you would most like to live in and explain why.

Chicago	Detroit	megalopolis	Seattle
South	terrorism	Washington, DC	

DIRECTIONS On the line provided before each statement, write **T** if a statement is true and **F** if a statement is false. If the statement is false, write the term from the word bank that would make the statement correct on the line after each sentence.

_____ 1. <u>Seattle</u> and New York are part of a megalopolis in the northeastern region of the United States.

_____

_____ 2. Most major cities in the Midwest, such as Detroit and <u>Chicago</u>, are located on rivers or the Great Lakes.

_____

_____ 3. The <u>South</u> includes coastlines along the Atlantic Ocean and the Gulf of Mexico.

_____

_____ 4. Terrorist acts in the United States have encouraged leaders around the world to work together to combat the problem of <u>terrorism</u>.

_____

_____ 5. Forestry and fishing are two important economic activities in the <u>Detroit</u> area.

_____

DIRECTIONS Choose four of the terms from the word bank. On a separate sheet of paper, use these terms to write a description of the United States.

Canada

> **MAIN IDEAS**
> 1. A huge country, Canada has a wide variety of physical features, including rugged mountains, plains, and swamps.
> 2. Because of its northerly location, Canada is dominated by cold climates.
> 3. Canada is rich in natural resources like fish, minerals, fertile soils, and forests.

Key Terms and Places

Rocky Mountains mountains that extend north from the United States into western Canada

St. Lawrence River important international waterway that links the Great Lakes to the Atlantic Ocean

Niagara Falls falls created by the waters of the Niagara River

Canadian Shield region of rocky uplands, lakes, and swamps

Grand Banks large fishing ground off the Atlantic coast near Newfoundland and Labrador

pulp softened wood fibers

newsprint cheap paper used mainly for newspapers

Lesson Summary
PHYSICAL FEATURES

Canada is the second-largest country in the world. Only Russia is larger. The United States and Canada share several physical features. Among them are the mountains along the Pacific coast and the **Rocky Mountains** as well as broad plains that stretch across both countries. The two nations also share a natural border formed by the **St. Lawrence River**.

Niagara Falls is another physical feature that the two countries share. The falls are created by the Niagara River as it drops over a rocky ledge.

One of Canada's unique features is the **Canadian Shield**. This rocky region covers about half of the country. Canadian territory extends north to the Arctic Ocean where the land is

> Underline the sentence that describes Canada's size compared to other countries in the world.

> List three physical features that are in both Canada and the United States.
> _____
> _____
> _____
> _____
> _____

covered with ice all year. Very few people live in this harsh environment.

CLIMATE

Canada's climate is greatly affected by its location. The country is far to the north of the equator. It is also at higher latitudes than the United States. Because of this, it generally has cool to freezing temperatures year round.

The coldest part of Canada is close to the Arctic Circle. Both central and northern Canada have subarctic climates. The far north has tundra and ice cap climates. More than 80 percent of Canadians live in urban areas. Many of these cities are located in provinces that border the United States, where the weather is relatively mild.

> How has Canada's location influenced its climate?
>
> _____
> _____
> _____
> _____
> _____

RESOURCES

Canada has many natural resources. These resources include fish, minerals, and forests. One of Canada's richest fishing areas is the **Grand Banks** near Newfoundland and Labrador, off the Atlantic coast. Large schools of fish once swam there, but too much fishing has reduced the number of fish in this part of the ocean.

Canada has many mineral resources. It also has oil and gas. Many of Canada's mineral resources come from the Canadian Shield, a region of rocky uplands, lakes, and swamps. Canada is a main source of the world's nickel, zinc, and uranium. Alberta produces most of Canada's oil and natural gas.

All across Canada, forests provide lumber and **pulp** to make paper. The United States, the United Kingdom, and Japan get much of their **newsprint** from Canada.

> Circle the names of three types of natural resources that Canada has.

CHALLENGE ACTIVITY

Critical Thinking: Draw Inferences How are Canada's natural resources connected to its climate and physical features? Write two paragraphs explaining the connections.

DIRECTIONS Read each sentence and fill in the blank with the word in the word pair that best completes the sentence.

1. The _____ forms a natural border between the United States and Canada. (**Canadian Shield/St. Lawrence River**)

2. _____ refers to softened wood fibers used to make paper. (**Pulp/Newsprint**)

3. The _____ extend from the western United States into western Canada. (**Grand Banks/Rocky Mountains**)

4. The Canadian Shield is a region of lakes, swamps, and rocky _____. (**tundra/uplands**)

5. _____ is a physical feature that the United States and Canada share. (**Hudson Bay/Niagara Falls**)

Canadian Shield	Grand Banks	Hudson Bay
newsprint	Niagara Falls	pulp
Rocky Mountains	St. Lawrence River	tundra
uplands		

DIRECTIONS Choose five of the terms from the word bank. Use these terms to write a summary of what you learned in the lesson.

_____

_____

_____

_____

_____

Canada

MAIN IDEAS

1. Beginning in the 1600s, Europeans settled the region that would later become Canada.
2. Immigration and migration to cities have shaped Canadian culture.

Key Terms and Places

Quebec province of Canada, first settled by the French

provinces administrative divisions of a country

British Columbia province of Canada on the Pacific Coast

Toronto Canada's largest city

Lesson Summary
HISTORY

Native peoples such as the Inuit were the first people to live in Canada. Over time, some of these native peoples divided into groups known as the First Nations. The Cree, one of those groups, lived on the plains. They survived by hunting bison. The Inuit lived in the far north. They learned to survive in the harsh, cold climate by hunting seals, whales, and other animals.

> Circle two groups that are part of the First Nations.

The Vikings were the first Europeans to come to Canada, but they did not stay. European explorers and fishermen came in the late 1400s. Europeans soon began to trade with Native Canadians. The French built the first permanent settlements in what became Canada. They called the lands they claimed New France. In the 1700s Britain defeated France in the French and Indian War. Although the British took control, most French settlers stayed. Their way of life did not change much. Many descendants of these French settlers live in **Quebec** today.

> How did the French and Indian War affect the French colonists in New France?
>
> _____
> _____
> _____

The British divided their territory into two colonies called Upper and Lower Canada. Canada stayed divided until 1867, when the

British passed a law making it a dominion, a territory or area of influence. This act gave Canada its own government. The British also divided the country into **provinces**. In 1885, Canadians completed a railroad across Canada. It connected **British Columbia** with the eastern provinces. Canada increased in size by buying lands in the north where many Native Canadians lived.

What is a dominion?
_____
_____

CULTURE

Canadians come from many places. Some are descendants of early settlers from France and Britain. In the late 1800s and early 1900s many immigrants came from Europe. Most were from Britain, Russia, and Germany. Some came from the United States. Most farmed, while others worked in mines, forests, and factories. Some hoped to find gold in Canada's Yukon Territory. Many Asian immigrants have come to Canada, especially from China, Japan, and India. Many Chinese immigrants came to work on the railroads. Immigrants helped Canada's economy grow. British Columbia was the first Canadian province to have a large Asian minority.

Circle the countries where some of Canada's immigrants came from prior to World War II.

After World War II a new wave of immigrants came to large cities like **Toronto**. Many came from Asia. Others came from Europe, Africa, the Caribbean, and Latin America. Like earlier immigrants, they came for jobs and new opportunities. In recent years, Canadians have also moved from farms in rural areas to large cities like Vancouver and Montreal. Many of these people have moved to cities to find jobs.

CHALLENGE ACTIVITY

Critical Thinking: Make Inferences How has immigration helped Canada's economy grow? Imagine that you are a person preparing to move to Canada. Write a letter to a friend explaining

your reasons for moving and how you expect to
contribute to the Canadian economy.

DIRECTIONS On the line provided before each statement, write **T** if
a statement is true and **F** if a statement is false. If the statement is
false, write the term that would make the statement correct on the
line after each sentence.

_____ 1. Since World War II, <u>Quebec</u> has become one of the most culturally
diverse cities in the world.

_____

_____ 2. Quebec and Ontario are examples of Canadian <u>colonies</u>.

_____

_____ 3. The Canadians built a transcontinental railroad to connect <u>British
Columbia</u> with eastern Canada.

_____

_____ 4. <u>Toronto</u> remains a mainly French-speaking region.

_____

_____ 5. A <u>dominion</u>, such as the Dominion of Canada, is a territory or area of
influence.

_____

DIRECTIONS Write three adjectives or descriptive phrases that
describe the term.

6. British Columbia _____

7. New France _____

8. Canadian Pacific Railroad _____

_____

9. Canadian Cities _____

10. First Nations _____

_____

Canada

Lesson 3

> **MAIN IDEAS**
> 1. Canada has a democratic government with a prime minister and a parliament.
> 2. Canada has four distinct geographic and cultural regions.
> 3. Canada's economy is largely based on trade with the United States.

Key Terms and Places

regionalism strong connection that people feel toward their region

maritime on or near the sea

Montreal Canada's second-largest city, one of the world's largest French-speaking cities

Ottawa Canada's national capital

Vancouver city on the Pacific coast with strong trade ties to Asia

Lesson Summary
CANADA'S GOVERNMENT

Canada has a democratic central government led by a prime minister. This job is like that of a president. The prime minister is the head of Canada's national government. The prime minister also leads Parliament, Canada's governing body. Parliament is made up of the House of Commons and the Senate. Canadians elect members of the House of Commons. The prime minister appoints senators. Provincial governments are like state governments. A premier leads each province.

> Circle the title of the person who is the leader of Canada's national government.

CANADA'S REGIONS

Canada has four regions. Each has its own cultural and physical features. In Quebec province, located in the Heartland region, **regionalism** has created problems between French and English speakers.

The Eastern Provinces are on the Atlantic coast region. They include three **Maritime** Provinces—

> Underline the names of the three Maritime Provinces.

Lesson 3, *continued*

New Brunswick, Nova Scotia and Prince Edward
Island—as well as Newfoundland and Labrador.
Most people live in cities near the coast. Forestry
and fishing are the major economic activities.

More than half of all Canadians live in the
Heartland region in the provinces of Ontario and
Quebec. This region includes **Montreal**, Toronto,
and **Ottawa**. Quebec is a center of French culture.
Ontario is Canada's top manufacturing province.

The Western region includes British Columbia
on the Pacific coast and the prairie provinces—
Manitoba, Saskatchewan, and Alberta. Farming
is important there, especially growing wheat. In
British Columbia, **Vancouver** is a major center for
trade with Asia.

The Canadian North region consists of the
Yukon and Northwest Territories and Nunavut,
the Inuit homeland. The region is very cold and
not many people live there. Nunavut has its own
local government.

> **List two ways in which the Eastern and Heartland provinces are different from each other.**
>
> _____
> _____
> _____
> _____
> _____
> _____
> _____
> _____
> _____
> _____
> _____
> _____

CANADA'S ECONOMY

Many of Canada's economic activities are
connected to its natural resources. Mining and
manufacturing are key industries along with
producing minerals. Most Canadians hold service
jobs. Tourism is the fastest-growing service
industry. Trade is also important. The United
States is Canada's leading trading partner. The
United States buys much of its lumber from
Canada.

> **Which type of economic activity employs the most workers?**
>
> _____
> _____

CHALLENGE ACTIVITY

Critical Thinking: Draw Conclusions Why do
you think Canada and the United States are
such strong trading partners? What are the
advantages and disadvantages of this strong
trading relationship? Explain your answer in a
one-page essay.

Guided Reading Workbook

Name _____ Class _____ Date _____

Lesson 3, *continued*

DIRECTIONS Look at each set of four vocabulary terms. On the line provided, write the letter of the term that does not relate to the others.

_____ 1. a. culture
      b. regionalism
      c. connection
      d. industrial

_____ 2. a. coast
      b. heartland
      c. Atlantic
      d. maritime

_____ 3. a. Montreal
      b. Toronto
      c. Ottawa
      d. Vancouver

_____ 4. a. Yukon
      b. Maritime
      c. Nunavut
      d. tundra

_____ 5. a. Alberta
      b. Manitoba
      c. Saskatchewan
      d. Nova Scotia

Heartland	Inuit	Maritime
Montreal	motto	Ottawa
Regionalism	Toronto	Vancouver

DIRECTIONS Choose five terms from the word bank. On the lines below use these terms to write a poem or story that relates to the lesson.

_____

_____

_____

_____

_____

_____

_____

Guided Reading Workbook

Early Civilizations of Latin America

MAIN IDEAS
1. The Olmec were the first complex civilization in Mesoamerica and influenced other cultures.
2. Geography helped shape the lives of the early Maya.
3. During the Classic Age, the Maya built great cities linked by trade.
4. Maya culture included a strict social structure, a religion with many gods, and achievements in science and the arts.
5. The decline of Maya civilization began in the 900s.

Key Terms and Places

civilization organized society within a specific area

maize corn

Palenque Maya city in which the king Pacal had a temple built to record his achievements

observatories buildings from which people could study the sky

Lesson Summary
THE OLMEC

Mesoamerica extends from central Mexico to the northern part of Central America. A people called the Olmec developed the first complex **civilization** in Mesoamerica around 1200 BC. The region is hot and humid with abundant rainfall and rich, fertile soil. The Olmec grew **maize**, beans, squash, peppers, and avocados.

> Underline the sentence that gives the location of Mesoamerica.

The Olmec built towns which were religious and government centers with temples and plazas. They built the first pyramids in the Americas and made sculptures of huge stone heads. They created one of the first writing systems in the Americas, but no one today knows how to read it. Their influence and culture spread through a large trading network. Olmec civilization ended around 400 BC, but it influenced the Maya.

> Why are there no translations of Olmec writing?
> _____
> _____
> _____

GEOGRAPHY AND THE EARLY MAYA

The Maya settled in thick tropical forests of what is now northern Guatemala. They cleared areas to farm beans, squash, avocados, and maize. The forests provided animals for food and plants for building materials. By AD 200, the Maya had begun building large cities in Mesoamerica.

What crops did the Maya grow?
_____
_____

THE CLASSIC AGE

Maya civilization was at its peak between AD 250 and 900, a period called the Classic Age. There were more than 40 Maya cities. These cities sometimes fought one another for control of land and resources. The Maya established trade routes throughout Mesoamerica and traded for the supplies they needed to build their grand cities.

The Maya built large stone pyramids, temples, palaces, and plazas. Some buildings honored local kings. A temple built in the city of **Palenque** (pah-LENG-kay) honored its builder, the king Pacal (puh-KAHL). The Maya built canals and shaped hillsides into flat terraces for crops. Volcanoes and volcanic eruptions influenced Maya civilization during this period.

How did Maya cities relate to one another?
_____
_____
_____
_____
_____
_____

How was the Maya king Pacal honored?
_____
_____

MAYA CULTURE

Social structure and religion were the main forces influencing Maya life. Kings held the highest position, both in politics and religion. Priests, warriors, and rich merchants were in the upper class. Most Maya belonged to lower class farming families. Maya farmers had to "pay" the rulers with some of their crops and with goods such as cloth and salt. They also had to help build temples and other buildings and serve in the army.

Which groups made up the upper class of the Maya social structure?
_____
_____

Guided Reading Workbook

Lesson 1, *continued*

The Maya worshipped many gods. They tried to keep their gods happy by giving them blood. They did this by piercing their tongues or skin. Maya achievements in art, architecture, math, science, and writing were remarkable. They built **observatories** for priests to study the stars. They developed a calendar that had 365 days. The Maya developed a writing system and a number system. They were among the first people with a symbol for zero.

> **What was special about the Maya number system?**
> _____
> _____

DECLINE OF MAYA CIVILIZATION

Maya civilization began to collapse in the AD 900s. They stopped building large structures and left the cities for the countryside. Historians are not sure why this happened, but there are several theories. Some historians believe that Maya farmers kept planting the same crop over and over, which weakened the soil. This may have caused more competition and war between the cities. The people may have decided to rebel against their kings' demands. Droughts may have played a part as well. There were probably many factors that led to the decline of the Maya civilization.

> **List two factors that may have contributed to the decline of the Maya civilization.**
> _____
> _____
> _____
> _____
> _____
> _____

CHALLENGE ACTIVITY

Critical Thinking: Make Inferences One source of information about the Maya comes from kings like Pacal, who dedicated a temple to his achievements. Draw a building that honors our culture. Include details that would help future historians reconstruct 21st century life.

DIRECTIONS Read each sentence and fill in the blank with the word in the word pair that best completes the sentence.

1. The Maya's religious beliefs led them to make impressive advances in science, using _____ to study astronomy. (**observatories/Palenque**)

2. The Maya grew a variety of crops, including _____, which is corn. (**avocados/maize**)

3. Pacal, a Maya king, had a temple built in _____ to honor his achievements. (**observatories/Palenque**)

4. The _____ developed the first complex civilization in Mesoamerica. (**Maya/Olmec**)

5. The Maya were influenced by Olmec _____. (**civilization/ Palenque**)

civilization	maize
Maya	observatories
Olmec	Palenque

DIRECTIONS Look up three terms from the word bank in an encyclopedia or dictionary. On a separate sheet of paper, write the encyclopedia or dictionary definition of the term that is closest to the definition used in your textbook. Then write a sentence using each term correctly.

Early Civilizations of Latin America

Lesson 2

MAIN IDEAS
1. The Aztecs built a rich and powerful empire in central Mexico.
2. Social structure, religion, and warfare shaped life in the empire.
3. Hernán Cortés conquered the Aztec Empire in 1521.

Key Terms and Places

Tenochtitlán island city and capital of the Aztec Empire

causeways raised roads across water or wet ground

conquistadors Spanish conquerors

Lesson Summary
THE AZTECS BUILD AN EMPIRE

The first Aztecs were farmers who migrated south to central Mexico. Other tribes had taken the good farmland, so the Aztecs settled on a swampy island in Lake Texcoco (tays-KOH-koh). In 1325, they began building their capital there.

War was key to the Aztecs' rise to power. The Aztec warriors conquered many towns and made the conquered people pay tribute with cotton, gold, or food. The Aztecs also controlled a large trade network.

The Aztecs' power and wealth was most visible in the capital, **Tenochtitlán** (tay-nawch-teet-LAHN). The Aztecs built three **causeways** to connect the island city to the lakeshore. They grew food on floating gardens, called *chinampas*. At its peak, Tenochtitlán had about 200,000 people. The city had temples, a palace, and a busy market.

> Why did the Aztecs settle on an island in Lake Texcoco?
> _____
> _____
> _____

> How were the Aztecs able to become wealthy?
> _____
> _____
> _____

LIFE IN THE EMPIRE

Aztec society had clearly defined social classes. The king was the most important person. He was in charge of law, trade, tribute, and warfare. The nobles, including tax collectors and judges,

> Underline the sentence that lists the responsibilities of the king.

helped the king with his duties. Below the king and nobles were priests and warriors. Priests had great influence over the Aztecs. Warriors were highly respected. Below priests and warriors were merchants and artisans, and then farmers and laborers. Slaves were lowest in society.

The Aztecs believed that gods ruled all parts of life and human sacrifice was necessary to keep the gods happy. In rituals, priests cut open victims' chests to give blood to the gods and sacrificed nearly 10,000 humans a year.

The Aztecs studied astronomy. Their calendar was much like the Maya calendar. The Aztecs had a rich artistic tradition and a writing system. They also had a strong oral tradition.

> **What did the Aztecs believe was necessary to keep the gods happy?**
>
> _____
> _____
> _____
> _____

CORTÉS CONQUERS THE AZTECS

In 1519 Hernán Cortés (er-NAHN kawr-TEZ) led a group of Spanish conquerors called **conquistadors** into Mexico. Their motives were to seek gold, claim land, and spread their religion. The Aztec ruler, Moctezuma II (MAWK-tay-SOO-mah), thought Cortés was a god. Moctezuma gave Cortés many gifts, including gold. Wanting more gold, Cortés took Moctezuma prisoner. Enraged, the Aztecs attacked the Spanish. They drove the Spanish out of the city, but Moctezuma was killed.

To defeat the Aztecs, the Spanish allied with people who did not like the Aztec rulers. The Spanish used guns and rode horses. They also carried diseases like smallpox that killed many Aztecs. In 1521 the Spanish brought the Aztec Empire to an end.

> **What factors contributed to the Aztecs' defeat?**
>
> _____
> _____
> _____
> _____

CHALLENGE ACTIVITY

Critical Thinking: Make Inferences Do you think
Cortés's actions toward the Aztecs were fair?
Write two paragraphs defending your opinion.
Give examples to support your opinion.

DIRECTIONS Write a word or phrase that explains the term or
name given.

1. Tenochtitlán _____

2. causeway _____

   _____

3. conquistadors _____

4. Hernán Cortés _____

5. Moctezuma II _____

6. tribute _____

7. chinampas _____

Early Civilizations of Latin America

> **MAIN IDEAS**
> 1. Prior to the Inca Empire, several civilizations grew in the Andes and along the Pacific coast of South America.
> 2. The Inca created an empire with a strong central government in South America.
> 3. Life in the Inca Empire was influenced by social structure, religion, and the Inca's cultural achievements.
> 4. Francisco Pizarro conquered the Inca and took control of the region in 1537.

Key Terms and Places

Cuzco capital of the Inca Empire, located in present-day Peru

Quechua official language of the Inca

masonry stonework

Lesson Summary
GEOGRAPHY AND EARLY ANDEAN CIVILIZATIONS

The Andes Mountains run along the western side of South America. Between the mountain ridges lie high plains, called *altiplano*. A narrow desert lies between the mountains and rich fishing waters in the Pacific Ocean. Rivers from the Andes drain into the Pacific and into the Amazon River to the east. The climate varies with latitude and altitude. Within this region, many civilizations grew, adapting to the land around them.

What is the *altiplano*?
_____
_____
_____

South America's first major civilization developed in what is now northern and central Peru. People of the Chavín culture grew maize and potatoes, wove textiles, carved stone monuments, and produced animal and human-shaped pottery. They were followed by the Moche in northern coastal Peru. The Moche irrigated their fields of corn, built adobe pyramids, and produced pottery and metalwork. Along the coast to the south, the Nazca used

Circle the names of the four early Andean civilizations.

Lesson 3, *continued*

irrigation to farm their dry region. They built
cisterns to hold water. Their artifacts include
large designs of animals, plants, and geometric
shapes which are best seen from the air. The
Chimú followed the Moche in northern coastal
Peru. They built irrigation systems, roads, and a
large capital. They were conquered by the Inca
around 1460.

THE INCA CREATE AN EMPIRE

The Inca began as a small tribe in the Andes.
They built their capital, **Cuzco**, in what is now
Peru. Inca territorial expansion began in the mid-
1400s under the ruler Pachacuti. By the early
1500s, the Inca Empire stretched from Ecuador
to central Chile.

> Underline the sentence that
> describes the Inca's
> beginnings.

To rule this vast empire, the Inca formed a
strong central government. The Inca replaced
local leaders of conquered areas with new people
loyal to the Inca government. The Inca
established an official language, **Quechua**. The
Inca paid taxes in the form of labor. This labor
tax system was called the *mita*. There were no
merchants or markets. Instead, government
officials would distribute goods collected through
the mita. Leftover goods were stored in the
capital for emergencies. If a natural disaster
struck, or if people simply could not care for
themselves, the government provided supplies to
help them.

> How did Inca get food,
> clothing, and other goods?
> _____
> _____
> _____
> _____
> _____

LIFE IN THE INCA EMPIRE

Inca society had two main social classes. The
emperor, priests, and government officials were
the upper class. The upper class lived in Cuzco
and did not pay the labor tax. The lower class
included farmers, artisans, and servants. Most
Inca were farmers. They grew maize and peanuts

Lesson 3, *continued*

in the warmer valleys and potatoes on terraced
hillsides in the mountains.

Inca religion was based on the belief that Inca
rulers were related to the sun god and never really
died. Inca ceremonies often included sacrifice of
llamas, cloth, or food. They also believed certain
natural landforms had magical powers.

To whom did the Inca believe their rulers were related?
_____
_____
_____

Inca are known for their expert **masonry**, or
stonework. They cut stone blocks so precisely
that no cement was needed to hold them
together. Some of their stone buildings and roads
have lasted until today. Inca artisans made
beautiful pottery, jewelry, and textiles. The Inca
had no written language, but they kept records
with knotted cords called *quipus*. They passed
down stories and songs orally.

The Inca excelled in the use of what building material?
_____
_____

PIZARRO CONQUERS THE INCA

In the late 1520s a civil war began between an
Inca ruler's two sons, Atahualpa and Huáscar.
Atahualpa won, but the war had weakened the
Inca army. On his way to be crowned king,
Atahualpa heard that conquistadors led by
Francisco Pizarro had arrived in the Inca Empire.
When Atahualpa came to meet them, the Spanish
captured him. They attacked and killed thousands
of Inca soldiers. Although the Inca brought gold
and silver to pay for Atahualpa's return, the
Spanish killed him. The Spanish defeated the Inca
and ruled their lands for the next 300 years.

Circle the name of the leader who led the Spanish conquistadors in their defeat of the Inca.

CHALLENGE ACTIVITY

Critical Thinking: Make Inferences The Inca used labor as a form of
taxation. Write two paragraphs explaining the advantages and
disadvantages of this practice.

DIRECTIONS Read each sentence and fill in the blank with the word in the word pair that best completes the sentence.

1. High plains, called _____, lie between the mountain ridges of the Andes. **(altiplano/mita)**

2. The Inca capital was called _____. **(Cuzco/Quechua)**

3. The _____ created large designs best seen from the air. **(Chimú/Nazca)**

4. The official language of the Inca was _____. **(quipu/Quechua)**

5. The _____, or Inca labor tax system, was not paid by the upper class. **(mita/masonry)**

DIRECTIONS Write a paragraph describing the Inca Empire using the words *Cuzco*, *Quechua*, and *masonry*.

Mexico

Lesson 1

MAIN IDEAS
1. Mexico's physical features include plateaus, mountains, and coastal lowlands.
2. Mexico's climate and vegetation include deserts, tropical forests, and cool highlands.
3. Key natural resources in Mexico include oil, silver, gold, and scenic landscapes.

Key Terms and Places

Río Bravo river, known in the United States as the Rio Grande, that forms part of Mexico's border with the United States

peninsula piece of land surrounded on three sides by water

Baja California peninsula stretching from northern Mexico into the Pacific Ocean

Yucatán Peninsula land separating the Gulf of Mexico from the Caribbean Sea

Gulf of Mexico body of water that forms Mexico's eastern border

Sierra Madre "mother range" made up of three mountain ranges in Mexico

Lesson Summary
PHYSICAL FEATURES

Mexico shares a long border with the United States. Part of this border is formed by a river called the **Río Bravo,** known as the Rio Grande in the United States. Mexico's western border is the Pacific Ocean, where a long **peninsula** called **Baja California** stretches south from northern Mexico. In the east, the **Yucatán Peninsula** separates the **Gulf of Mexico** from the Caribbean Sea.

> Underline the names of Mexico's two peninsulas.

The interior of Mexico is mostly the high, rugged Mexican Plateau, which rises in the west to the Sierra Madre Occidental. In the east it meets the Sierra Madre Oriental. **Sierra Madre** means "mother range." The country's capital, Mexico City, lies at the southern end of the plateau in the Valley of Mexico. The city has earthquakes, and to the south there are active volcanoes.

> Where is Mexico City located?
> _____
> _____

From the central highlands, the land slopes down to Mexico's sunny beaches. In the east the Gulf coastal plain is wide, and there are many farms.

The Yucatán Peninsula is mostly flat. The limestone rock there has eroded to form caves and steep depressions called sinkholes, many of which are filled with water.

> **How is the terrain in the Yucatán Peninsula different from that of the Sierra Madre?**
>
> _____
>
> _____

CLIMATE AND VEGETATION

Mexico has many climates with different types of vegetation. The mountains and plateaus are cool, and freezing temperatures can reach all the way to Mexico City. The mountain valleys are mild, and the southern coast is also pleasant. Summer rains support tropical rain forests, where animals such as jaguars, monkeys, and anteaters live. The Yucatán Peninsula is hot and dry, supporting only scrub forests. The north is also dry, much of it covered by desert.

> **Underline the words that describe the many climates of Mexico.**

NATURAL RESOURCES

Petroleum, or oil, is an important resource. Mexico sells a lot of oil to the United States. Before oil was discovered, minerals were the most valuable resource. Today, Mexico mines more silver than any other country. Copper, lead, gold, and zinc are also mined.

Another important resource is water. Unfortunately, this resource is scarce in many parts of Mexico. However, the water surrounding Mexico draws many tourists to the country's scenic beaches.

> **What is Mexico's most important mineral product?**
>
> _____

CHALLENGE ACTIVITY

Critical Thinking: Make Predictions Write a paragraph making a prediction about which of Mexico's resources will be most important in Mexico's future. Support your prediction with information you learned in the lesson.

Guided Reading Workbook

Name _____ Class _____ Date _____

DIRECTIONS On the line provided before each statement, write **T** if
a statement is true and **F** if a statement is false. If a statement is
false, write the term that would make the statement correct on the
line after each sentence.

_____ 1. In the Yucatán Peninsula, erosion of limestone rock has created many
caves and <u>sinkholes</u>.

_____

_____ 2. The climate in southern Mexico is mostly warm and humid, or
<u>peninsula.</u>

_____

_____ 3. Baja California is a narrow <u>plateau</u> that stretches into the Pacific
Ocean.

_____

_____ 4. <u>Petroleum</u> is one of Mexico's most important natural resources.

_____

_____ 5. The <u>Gulf of Mexico</u> is Mexico's eastern border.

_____

DIRECTIONS Write three words or phrases that describe the term.

6. peninsula _____

7. Río Bravo _____

8. plateau _____

9. Sierra Madre _____

10. Yucatán Peninsula _____

Mexico

MAIN IDEAS

1. Early cultures of Mexico included the Olmecs, the Mayas, and the Aztecs.
2. Mexico's period as a Spanish colony and its struggles since independence have shaped its culture.
3. Spanish and native cultures have influenced Mexico's customs and traditions today.

Key Terms and Places

empire land with different territories and peoples under a single ruler

mestizos Spanish name for people of mixed European and Indian ancestry

mulattoes Spanish name for people of mixed European and African ancestry

missions church outposts

haciendas huge expanses of farm or ranch land

Lesson Summary
EARLY CULTURES

People of Mexico grew corn, beans, peppers, and squash as early as 5,000 years ago. Around 1500 BC the Olmecs settled on the southern coast of the Gulf of Mexico. They built temples and statues. About AD 250 the Mayas built cities in Mexico and Central America. They were astronomers and left written records. Maya civilization collapsed after AD 900.

> Circle the achievements of the Olmecs and Mayas.

Later, the Aztecs moved into central Mexico. In 1325 they founded their capital, Tenochtitlán. They built an **empire** through conquest of other tribes.

COLONIAL MEXICO AND INDEPENDENCE

In 1519 a Spanish soldier, Hernán Cortés, arrived in Mexico with guns, horses, and about 600 soldiers. The Spanish also brought diseases that killed many Aztecs. This helped Cortés defeat the Aztecs in 1521.

> How long did it take Cortés to conquer the Aztecs?
> _____

Many people in colonial Mexico were of mixed European and Indian ancestry and were called **mestizos**. When Africans were brought to America as slaves, they added to the mix of people. The Spaniards called people of mixed European and African ancestry **mulattoes**. The Catholic Church was important in the colony. Priests tried to convert the Indians, traveling far north to build **missions**.

Spain was eager to mine gold and silver in Mexico. The native people and enslaved Africans did most of the mining. They also worked the huge farms and ranches, called **haciendas**, that were owned by wealthy people of Spanish ancestry.

> **Who owned the haciendas?**
> _____
> _____

Mexico gained independence in 1821. Miguel Hidalgo started the revolt in 1810 by asking for equality. Later, Texas broke away from Mexico and joined the United States. The two countries fought over their border in the Mexican-American War. Mexico lost the war and almost half its territory.

In the mid-1800s, the popular president Benito Juárez made many reforms. But in the early 1900s the government helped the hacienda owners take land from the peasants. People were angry and started the Mexican Revolution in 1910. In 1920 a new government took land from the large landowners and gave it back to the peasants.

> **What did the government do that made people angry?**
> _____
> _____
> _____

CULTURE

In Mexico language is tied to ethnic groups. Speaking an American Indian language identifies a person as Indian. Mexicans have combined Indian religious practices with Catholic practices. One example is a holiday called Day of the Dead. On this day, Mexicans follow native traditions for remembering ancestors. The holiday is celebrated on November 1 and 2—the same dates as similar Catholic holidays.

> **Underline the Indian aspects of the Day of the Dead**

CHALLENGE ACTIVITY

Critical Thinking: Sequence Make a timeline with important dates and events in Mexican history.

DIRECTIONS Read each sentence and circle the word in the word pair that best completes each sentence.

1. Through conquest of neighboring tribes, the (**Olmec/Aztecs**) built an empire.

2. The term that the Spanish used for people in colonial Mexico with both European and Indian ancestry was (**mestizos/mulattoes**).

3. During colonial times, Catholic priests at (**haciendas/missions**) taught the Indians Spanish and learned their language.

4. To seek independence from Spain, Miguel Hidalgo began a/an (**revolt/empire**) in 1810.

DIRECTIONS Look at each set of four vocabulary terms. On the line provided, write the letter of the term that does not relate to the others.

_____ 5. a. haciendas   _____ 6. a. ancestors
         b. ranches   b. Day of the Dead
         c. peasants   c. chinampas
         d. mulattoes   d. celebration

chinampas	conquistadors	empire	haciendas
mestizos	missions	mulattoes	revolt

DIRECTIONS Choose five of the words from the word bank. On a separate sheet of paper, use these words to write a summary of what you have learned in the lesson.

Mexico

MAIN IDEAS
1. Government has traditionally played a large role in Mexico's economy.
2. Mexico has four distinct culture regions.

Key Terms and Places

inflation rise in prices that occurs when currency loses its buying power

indigenous original or native resident of a specific region

slash-and-burn agriculture practice of burning forest to clear land for planting

cash crop crop that farmers grow mainly to sell for a profit

Mexico City world's second-largest city and Mexico's capital

smog mixture of smoke, chemicals, and fog

maquiladoras U.S.- and foreign-owned factories in Mexico

Lesson Summary
GOVERNMENT

Mexico's government has made improvements over the years. Today people in Mexico can vote in certain elections. People can find jobs in cities and buy a home. More children can attend school. However, that was not always true. Although Mexico is a democracy, one political party ran the government for 71 years. This ended in 2000 when Vicente Fox was elected president. He represented a different political party.

> Underline the improvements people in Mexico enjoy today.
> _____

ECONOMY

Like other developing countries, Mexico has foreign debts, unemployment, and **inflation**. Due to the North American Free Trade Agreement (NAFTA), Mexico now sells more products to the United States and Canada. Although exports have helped the economy, some Mexicans believe NAFTA has not helped the **indigenous** people, or

> How did NAFTA change trade for Mexico?
> _____
> _____
> _____

native Indians, who mostly farm on communal lands.

Agriculture is a key part of the Mexican economy. Some farmers who do not own much land and only grow enough to feed their families use **slash-and-burn agriculture**. Other farmers specialize by growing **cash crops**, such as fruits and vegetables. Trucks often bring these cash crops to the United States.

Mexicans work in oil fields and in factories. Many Mexicans also come to the United States looking for work. Tourists visit Mexico to enjoy its attractions.

MEXICO'S CULTURE REGIONS

Mexico has four culture regions that differ from one another in population, resources, and climate.

The Greater **Mexico City** region includes the capital and about 50 nearby cities. More than 19 million people make Mexico City one of the world's largest cities. Many people move there to look for work, and air pollution has become a problem. The mountains trap the **smog**—a mixture of smoke, chemicals, and fog. Poverty is also a problem.

Many cities in Mexico's central region were colonial mining or ranching centers. Mexico's colonial heritage can be seen today in the churches and public squares of this region. Family farmers grow vegetables and corn in the fertile valleys. In recent years, cities such as Guadalajara have attracted new industries from Mexico City.

> Underline information about the current economy of Mexico's central region. Circle information about its past economy.

Trade with the United States has helped northern region cities like Monterrey and Tijuana grow. Foreign-owned factories, called **maquiladoras**, have been built in this region. Many Mexicans cross the border to shop, work, or live in the United States. Some cross the

> What has helped Monterrey and Tijuana grow?
>
> _____
>
> _____

border legally. The U.S. government tries to
prevent illegal immigration.

Many people in the southern Mexico region
speak Indian languages and follow traditional
customs. Sugarcane and coffee, two major export
crops, grow well in the humid southern climate.
Oil production in the region has brought
population growth to southern Mexico. Maya
ruins, sunny beaches, and clear blue waters make
tourism a major industry in the Yucatán
Peninsula. Many of today's cities were tiny
villages just 20 years ago.

> Underline information
> about the people in
> Mexico's southern region.

CHALLENGE ACTIVITY

Critical Thinking: Compare and Contrast Make a
four-columned chart—one column for each
cultural region in Mexico. Make three rows and
write information for each region about History,
Population and Economy, and Geography and
Natural Resources. When you have completed the
chart, circle items that are similar among the
regions.

cash crop	indigenous	inflation
maquiladoras	Mexico City	slash-and-burn agriculture
smog		

DIRECTIONS Answer each question by writing a sentence that
contains at least one term from the word bank.

1. How has Mexico's economy struggled?

_____

_____

_____

2. Why is northern Mexico's economy growing today?

_____

_____

_____

3. Why were some Mexicans unhappy with the North American Free Trade Agreement (NAFTA)?

_____

_____

_____

4. What types of agriculture do farmers practice in southern Mexico?

_____

_____

_____

DIRECTIONS Your family is planning a trip to Mexico City. On a separate sheet of paper, write a paragraph describing what you expect to see when you get there.

Central America and the Caribbean

MAIN IDEAS
1. Physical features of the region include volcanic highlands and coastal plains.
2. The climate and vegetation of the region include forested highlands, tropical forests, and humid lowlands.
3. Key natural resources in the region include rich soils for agriculture, a few minerals, and beautiful beaches.

Key Terms and Places

isthmus narrow strip of land that connects two larger land areas

Caribbean Sea sea surrounded by Central America, the Greater and Lesser Antilles, and South America

Lesser Antilles group of small islands in the Caribbean Sea

archipelago large group of islands

Greater Antilles group of large islands in the Caribbean Sea

cloud forest moist, high-elevation tropical forest where low clouds are common

Lesson Summary
PHYSICAL FEATURES

Central America is an **isthmus** that connects North and South America. It is made up of seven small countries: Belize, Guatemala, El Salvador, Honduras, Nicaragua, Costa Rica, and Panama. At its widest, the isthmus separates the Pacific Ocean and the **Caribbean Sea** by 125 miles (200 km). A chain of mountains and volcanoes runs through the middle of the isthmus. On both sides, a few short rivers run through the coastal plains to the sea. The lack of good water routes and ruggedness of the land make travel difficult.

The Caribbean islands separate the Atlantic Ocean from the Caribbean Sea. On the east lie the **Lesser Antilles**, an **archipelago** of islands that stretch from the Virgin Islands to Trinidad and Tobago. West and north of these are the **Greater Antilles**, which include Cuba, Jamaica, Puerto Rico, and Hispaniola. The Bahama Islands,

> Underline the names of the seven countries that make up Central America.

> What two bodies of water are separated by the Caribbean islands?
>
> _____
> _____

located in the Atlantic Ocean, southeast of Florida, include nearly 700 islands and thousands of reefs. Many of these islands are actually the tops of underwater volcanoes. They are located along the edges of tectonic plates that move against each other, causing earthquakes and volcanic eruptions.

What causes earthquakes and volcanoes in the region?
_____
_____
_____

CLIMATE AND VEGETATION

Most of the region is generally sunny and warm. Most of Central America's Pacific coast, where plantations and ranches are found, has a tropical savanna climate. The Caribbean coast has areas of tropical rain forest. The inland mountains are cool and humid. Some mountainous areas have dense **cloud forests**, or moist, high-elevation tropical forests where low clouds are common. Many animal and plant species live there.

Where are cloud forests found?
_____
_____

Temperatures in the region do not change much from day to night or from winter to summer. Change in seasons is marked by changes in rainfall. Winters are generally dry, but it rains nearly every day in the summer. From summer to fall, hurricanes bring heavy rains and wind, which occasionally cause flooding and great destruction.

RESOURCES

The region's best resources are its land and climate, which make tourism an important industry. Warm climate and rich volcanic soil make the region a good place to grow coffee, bananas, sugarcane, and cotton. However, the region has few mineral or energy resources.

What two factors make the region a good place to grow crops?
_____
_____

CHALLENGE ACTIVITY

Critical Thinking: Compare and Contrast Write a description of the year-round climate in your region and compare and contrast it with that of the Central American and Caribbean region.

DIRECTIONS Read each sentence and fill in the blank with the word in the word pair that best completes the sentence.

1. The land that the seven countries of Central America are on is an _____, a narrow strip of land that connects two larger land areas. (**archipelago/isthmus**)

2. A large group of islands, such as the Caribbean Islands, is called an _____. (**archipelago/isthmus**)

3. The _____ is the body of water between Central America and the Caribbean Islands. (**Greater Antilles/Caribbean Sea**)

4. Cuba is part of the _____, one of the two main island groups in the Caribbean. (**Greater Antilles/Caribbean Sea**)

5. The many smaller islands of the Caribbean are called the _____. (**Lesser Antilles/Greater Antilles**)

6. A _____ is a moist, high-elevation tropical forest where low clouds are common. (**cloud forest/tropical savanna**)

archipelago	Caribbean Sea	cloud forest	Greater Antilles
isthmus	Lesser Antilles	reefs	volcanic ash

DIRECTIONS On a separate sheet of paper, write a letter to someone who lives in a desert region. Describe how the geography of the Central America and Caribbean area differs from the desert. Include at least four terms from the word bank to describe the Central America and Caribbean region.

Guided Reading Workbook

Central America and the Caribbean

> **MAIN IDEAS**
> 1. The history of Central America was mostly influenced by Spain.
> 2. The culture of Central America is a mixture of Native American and European traditions.
> 3. Today, the countries of Central America have challenges and opportunities.

Key Terms and Places

civil war conflict between two or more groups within a country

ecotourism practice of using an area's natural environment to attract tourists

Panama Canal waterway connecting the Pacific Ocean, the Caribbean Sea, and the Atlantic Ocean

Lesson Summary
HISTORY

The Maya people built a civilization in the region from about AD 250 to 900. Many of their descendants, and some of their customs, can still be found. In the 1500s Spain controlled the entire region except for Belize, which became a British colony. The Europeans established gold mines and large tobacco and sugarcane plantations and forced the Central American Indians to do the hard work. They also brought enslaved Africans to work.

> Underline the country that controlled most of the region in the 1500s.

In 1821 Honduras, El Salvador, Costa Rica, Guatemala, and Nicaragua gained independence and were a single country until 1839. Panama was part of Colombia until 1903. Belize separated from Britain in 1981. Independence did not help most people, as wealthy landowners took control. In the early to mid-1900s the U.S.-based United Fruit Company controlled most of the banana production in the region. Many people resented the role of foreign companies and thought it was unfair for a few people to have so much power. In the mid- to late 1900s

> Underline the sentence that explains why people in the region objected to large foreign companies.

people fought for land reform in Guatemala, El Salvador, and Nicaragua.

CULTURE

Most people in Central America are mestizos, people of mixed Indian and European ancestry. Some Indian people live in areas such as the highlands, and people of African ancestry live mainly along the eastern coast. English is the official language in Belize. Spanish is also spoken there and in the other countries. Many people speak Indian languages.

> Underline the languages that are spoken in the region.

The Spanish brought Roman Catholicism to people in the region, but Indian traditions are also followed. Corn, tomatoes, chocolate, and hot peppers are foods of the region.

CENTRAL AMERICA TODAY

Guatemala has the region's largest population. Most people are mestizos, but many are descendants of the Mayas. Conflict there killed some 200,000 people from 1960 to 1996. Coffee is the most important crop.

Honduras is mountainous, making transportation difficult. It has little farmland, but fruit is exported.

In the 1980s the poor people of El Salvador fought a **civil war** against the few rich families that owned much of the best land, which is very fertile. The war ended in 1992, and people are rebuilding.

> Underline the countries that fought a civil war in the last century.

Nicaragua was ruled by Sandinistas from 1979 to 1990. After a civil war, it became a democracy.

Costa Rica has been more peaceful than most of its neighbors, which helps its economy. Coffee, bananas, and tourism are its largest industries.

Belize has the region's lowest population. Recently, **ecotourism** has become a large industry, as more people visit the Maya ruins and coral reefs.

> Which country has been more peaceful than most of the other countries in the region?
>
> _____

Most Panamanians live near the **Panama Canal**, built and controlled by the United States. In 1999 the United States gave control to Panama.

CHALLENGE ACTIVITY

Critical Thinking: Sequence Make a timeline that shows important events in Central American history.

DIRECTIONS On the line before each statement, write **T** if the statement is true and **F** if the statement is false. If the statement is false, change the underlined term to make the sentence true. Then write the correct term on the line after the sentence.

_____ 1. The <u>Europeans</u> began building large cities with pyramids and temples in many Central American countries.

_____

_____ 2. Most of Central America came under the control of Europeans, who established <u>ecotourism</u> to grow crops such as tobacco and sugarcane.

_____

_____ 3. The Spanish colonies declared <u>independence</u> from Spain, but little changed, leading to wars more than a century later.

_____

_____ 4. As agreed to with the United States, Panama took over the <u>Maya,</u> which links the Pacific Ocean, Caribbean Sea, and Atlantic Ocean.

_____

_____ 5. Belize is one country that supports its economy with <u>plantations,</u> using its natural environment to attract tourists.

_____

civil wars	ecotourism	Europeans	independence
Mayas	Panama Canal	plantations	

DIRECTIONS Write a poem or short story about the history or culture of Central America. Use at least four terms from the word bank.

Central America and the Caribbean

Lesson 3

MAIN IDEAS
1. The history of the Caribbean islands includes European colonization followed by independence.
2. The culture of the Caribbean islands shows signs of past colonialism and slavery.
3. Today the Caribbean islands have distinctive governments with economies that depend on agriculture and tourism.

Key Terms and Places

Columbian Exchange movement of people, animals, plants, ideas, and diseases between Europe and the Americas

dialect regional variety of a language

commonwealth self-governing territory associated with another country

refugee someone who flees to another country, usually for political or economic reasons

Havana capital of Cuba

cooperative organization owned by its members and operated for their benefit

Lesson Summary

HISTORY

The Caribbean islands were the first land Christopher Columbus saw in 1492, though he thought he had sailed to islands near India. By the 1700s the islands were colonized by the Spanish, English, French, Dutch, and Danish. They brought enslaved Africans to work on their sugarcane plantations.

> Underline the sentence that tells who colonized the Caribbean islands.

Much of the sugar grown in this area was exported to Europe, along with other crops. Colonists then imported products, food, and even animals from Europe. This movement of people, animals, plants, ideas, and diseases between Europe and the Americas came to be known as the **Columbian Exchange**.

Lesson 3, *continued*

Haiti gained independence in 1804. Cuba became independent in 1902. Other islands became independent after World War II. Some, such as Martinique and Guadeloupe, never did. Most people on these French islands do not want independence.

CULTURE

Most islanders are descended from Europeans, Africans, or a mixture of the two. There are also some Asians. Some people speak English, French, or Spanish—others speak Creole, a **dialect**, or regional variety of a language.

Today, islands colonized by France and Spain have many Catholics. Elsewhere, people practice a blend of Catholicism and traditional African religion called Santería. Caribbean people enjoy the Carnival holiday. It comes before the Christian season of Lent and features parades and costumes. Some of the region's foods, such as okra and yams, were brought to the area by enslaved Africans. They also made souse, a dish made from the leftover pork given to them by slaveholders.

THE CARIBBEAN ISLANDS TODAY

Puerto Rico is a **commonwealth**, a self-governing territory associated with the United States. Some Puerto Ricans are happy about this, while others would like to become a state or a separate country. Though richer than others in the region, Puerto Ricans are not as well off as other U.S. citizens.

Haiti, occupying the western part of Hispaniola, is the poorest country in the Americas. Dishonest governments have caused violence, which many Haitians have tried to escape by becoming **refugees**.

> Underline the sentence that describes the general economic status of people living in Puerto Rico.

> What is the poorest country in the Americas?
> _____

Guided Reading Workbook

Lesson 3, *continued*

The eastern part of Hispaniola is the Dominican Republic. Its industries are tourism and agriculture.

Havana is the capital of Cuba, the largest, most populous island in the Caribbean. Cuba has been run by a Communist government since Fidel Castro came to power in 1959. The government runs the economy, newspapers, and television. Most farms are organized as **cooperatives**, owned by the people who work on them and run for their benefit.

> Underline the sentences that describe Cuba's government.

Some of the remaining Caribbean islands, such as Jamaica, are independent countries. Others, such as the Virgin Islands, are territories of other countries. Most rely on tourism for their income.

CHALLENGE ACTIVITY

Critical Thinking: Make Inferences Imagine you are a Haitian refugee. Write a paragraph describing the reasons you left Haiti and your hopes for the future.

DIRECTIONS Look at each set of words. On the line provided, write the letter of the term that does not relate to the others.

_____ 1. a. dialect   b. language   c. religion   d. Creole

_____ 2. a. treasury   b. territory   c. Puerto Rico   d. commonwealth

_____ 3. a. refugee   b. poverty   c. tourism   d. violence

_____ 4. a. Hispaniola   b. Havana   c. Cuba   d. Castro

_____ 5. a. cooperative   b. territory   c. members   d. organization

_____ 6. a. Columbian Exchange b. movement   c. people   d. dialect

| Columbian Exchange | commonwealth | cooperative | dialect |
| Havana | Hispaniola | refugee | revolt |

DIRECTIONS Write a summary of what you learned in Lesson 3. Use five of the terms from the word bank.

_____

_____

_____

_____

_____

_____

_____

South America

MAIN IDEAS
1. Coastal lowlands, mountains and highlands, and river systems shape much of Caribbean South America.
2. Atlantic South America's rain forests are its major source of natural resources.
3. The Andes mountains are Pacific South America's main physical feature.

Key Terms and Places

Andes mountains on the western side of Colombia

cordillera mountain system made up of roughly parallel ranges

Llanos plains region between the highlands and Andes

Orinoco River longest river in the region, flows through Venezuela to the Atlantic Ocean

Amazon River 4,000-mile-long river that flows eastward across northern Brazil

estuary partially enclosed body of water where freshwater mixes with salty seawater

Río de la Plata estuary that connects the Paraná River and the Atlantic Ocean

Pampas wide, grassy plains in central Argentina

deforestation action of clearing trees

soil exhaustion soil that has become infertile because it has lost nutrients needed by plants

altiplano broad, high plateau that lies between the ridges of the Andes

El Niño ocean weather pattern that affects the Pacific coast

Lesson Summary
CARIBBEAN SOUTH AMERICA

Caribbean South America includes rugged mountains, highlands, and plains drained by huge river systems. The region's highest point is in western Colombia, where the snow-capped **Andes** reach 18,000 feet. These mountains form a **cordillera**, or a system of roughly parallel mountain ranges. The **Llanos** is mostly grassland

> Underline the sentence that describes the Llanos.

and often floods. The **Orinoco River** and its tributaries drain the plains and highlands. Two other rivers, the Cauca and the Magdalena, drain the Andean region.

Most of the region is warm year round since it is near the equator. However, higher elevations are cooler. The grassy Llanos has low elevation. It has a tropical savanna climate with wet and dry seasons. Humid tropical rain forests cover much of southern Colombia. Heavy rainfall produces huge trees and vegetation so thick that sunlight barely reaches the jungle floor. Resources include agriculture, oil, timber, and plentiful hydroelectric power.

> **Describe the climate of southern Colombia.**
> _____
> _____
> _____

ATLANTIC SOUTH AMERICA

The Atlantic South America region includes Brazil, Argentina, Uruguay, and Paraguay. The **Amazon River** extends from the Andes Mountains in Peru to the Atlantic Ocean. The Paraná River drains much of the central part of South America. It flows into an **estuary** called the **Río de la Plata** and the Atlantic Ocean. The region's landforms mainly consist of plains and plateaus. The Amazon Basin in northern Brazil is a huge, flat floodplain. Farther south are the Brazilian Highlands and an area of high plains called the Mato Grosso Plateau. The low plains region, Gran Chaco, stretches across parts of Paraguay and northern Argentina. The grassy plains of the **Pampas** are found in central Argentina. Patagonia is a region of dry plains and plateaus south of the Pampas. These plains rise in the west to form the Andes Mountains.

> **Underline the names of four plains regions in Atlantic South America.**

Atlantic South America has many climates. Southern and highland areas tend to have cool climates. Northern and coastal areas generally have tropical and moist climates. The Amazon rain forest provides food, wood, rubber, plants for medicines, and other products. **Deforestation**

> **What threatens this region?**
> _____
> _____

threatens the resources of the rain forest. Land near the coastal areas in the region is used for commercial farming but some areas face **soil exhaustion**. Other resources include gold, silver, copper, iron, oil, and hydroelectric power from the rivers.

PACIFIC SOUTH AMERICA

The Andes Mountains run through all of the Pacific South American countries. In the south, the mountains are rugged and covered by ice caps. In the north, they are rounded and the range splits into two ridges. A high plateau, called the **altiplano**, lies between the two ridges. Rivers flowing into the altiplano never reach the sea, but fill two large lakes. At the southern tip of the continent, the Strait of Magellan links the Atlantic and Pacific oceans.

Climate, vegetation, and landscapes all vary widely in Pacific South America. In this region, elevation has the biggest effect on climate and vegetation. Bananas and sugarcane are grown in the hot and humid elevations near sea level and in the Amazon basin. In the moist climates of the mountain forests, coffee is grown. In the forests and grasslands, potatoes and wheat are grown. At the higher altitudes, vegetation is limited. In the Atacama Desert of northern Chile, rain falls only about once every 20 years. A recurring weather pattern called **El Niño** causes extreme and unusual weather around the world. The region's natural resources include lumber, gold and other metals, and oil and natural gas. The lack of good farmland means there are few agricultural exports.

> Underline the sentences that compare the Andes Mountains in the south and in the north.

> What is the main reason climate varies in the region?
>
> _____

CHALLENGE ACTIVITY
**Critical Thinking: Compare and
Contrast** Compare the resources of the three
regions of South America. How are they similar
and how are they different?

DIRECTIONS Read each sentence and fill in the blank with the word
in the word pair that best completes the sentence.

1. The Andes mountains form a _____, or system of roughly

    parallel mountain ranges. (**cordillera/estuary**)

2. The _____ extends from the Andes Mountains in Peru to the

    Atlantic Ocean. (**Amazon River/Orinoco River**)

3. An _____ is a partially enclosed body of water where freshwater

    and seawater mix. (**altiplano/estuary**)

4. The _____ are grassy plains of central Argentina.

    (**Llanos/Pampas**)

5. _____, a recurring weather pattern, causes extreme and unusual

    weather around the world. (**El Niño/Río de la Plata**)

6. The _____ is a high plateau between the two ridges of the An-

    des. (**altiplano/cordillera**)

altiplano	Amazon River	Andes	cordillera
deforestation	El Niño	estuary	Llanos
Orinoco River	Pampas	Río de la Plata	soil exhaustion

DIRECTIONS Answer each question by writing a sentence that contains at least two terms from the word bank.

7. Into what body of water does the Paraná River flow?

_____

8. What problems are affecting the natural resources of Atlantic South America?

_____

_____

South America

Lesson 2

| **MAIN IDEAS** |
| 1. Brazil's history has been affected by Brazilian Indians, Portuguese settlers, and enslaved Africans. |
| 2. Brazil's society reflects a mix of people and cultures. |
| 3. Brazil today is experiencing population growth in its cities and new development in rain forest areas. |

Key Terms and Places

São Paulo largest urban area in South America, located in southeastern Brazil

megacity giant urban area that includes surrounding cities and suburbs

Rio de Janeiro Brazil's second-largest city, located northeast of São Paulo

favelas huge slums

Brasília capital of Brazil

Manaus major port and industrial city, located 1,000 miles from the mouth of the Amazon River

Lesson Summary
HISTORY

Brazil is the largest country in South America. It has a population of more than 211 million people. The first people in Brazil were American Indians who arrived in the region thousands of years ago.

In 1500 Portuguese explorers became the first Europeans to find Brazil. Colonists brought Africans to the region to work as slaves on sugar plantations. These plantations helped make Portugal rich.

Gold and precious gems were discovered in the late 1600s and early 1700s in the southeast. The resulting mining boom drew people to Brazil from all over the world. Brazil became a major coffee producer in the late 1800s. Brazil gained independence from Portugal without a fight in 1822. Since the end of Portuguese rule, Brazil has been governed by both dictators and elected

| Who were the first people to live in Brazil? |
| _____ |

| What discovery brought people to Brazil from all over the world? |
| _____ |

officials. Today Brazil has an elected president
and legislature.

PEOPLE AND CULTURE

Nearly 40 percent of Brazil's people are of mixed
African and European descent. Brazil also has
the largest Japanese population outside of Japan.
Brazil's official language is Portuguese.

Brazil has the world's largest population of
Roman Catholics. Some Brazilians practice
macumba, a religion that combines beliefs and
practices of African and Indian religions with
Christianity.

Brazilians celebrate Carnival, a celebration
that mixes traditions from Africa, Brazil, and
Europe.

What percentage of Brazil's people are of mixed African and European descent?
_____

What is macumba?
_____
_____
_____
_____

BRAZIL TODAY

Brazil can be divided into four regions. The
southeast is the most populated. About
21 million people live in and around the city of
São Paulo. São Paulo is considered a **megacity**,
or giant urban area that includes surrounding
cities and suburbs. **Rio de Janeiro**, Brazil's former
capital and second-largest city, is also located in
the southeast. The southeast has a good
economy, but it also has poverty. Many people
live in city slums, or **favelas**.

The northeast is Brazil's poorest region.
Drought has made farming difficult. However,
many tourists are attracted to the region.
Tourism is an important industry.

The interior region is a frontier land, with
much potential for farming. The capital of
Brazil, **Brasília**, was built there in the mid-1950s.

The Amazon region covers the northern part
of Brazil. **Manaus** is a major port and industrial
city 1,000 miles from the mouth of the Amazon
River. The Amazon rain forest is a valuable
resource to people who live and work there, but

What is Brazil's second-largest city?
_____

Circle the word describing an important industry in northeast Brazil.

What are the four regions of Brazil?
_____
_____
_____

deforestation threatens the wildlife and Brazilian
Indians living there.

CHALLENGE ACTIVITY

Critical Thinking: Draw Conclusions Why do
most Brazilians live in the southeast? Write a
paragraph to explain your answer.

Brasília	Carnival	favelas
macumba	Manaus	megacity
Rio de Janeiro	São Paulo	

DIRECTIONS Read each sentence and choose the correct term from
the word bank to replace the underlined phrase. Write the term in
the space provided and then define the term in your own words.

1. This city was built in the interior region in the mid-1950s. _____

   Your definition: _____

   _____

2. These areas within Brazil's southeastern cities are marked by poverty.

   _____

   Your definition: _____

   _____

3. This cultural event mixes traditions from Africa, Brazil, and Europe.

   _____

   Your definition: _____

   _____

4. Popular with tourists, <u>this major port city</u> was once Brazil's capital.

_____

Your definition: _____

_____

5. São Paulo is a <u>giant city</u>. _____

_____

Your definition: _____

_____

_____

Lesson 3

MAIN IDEAS
1. European immigrants have dominated the history and culture of Argentina.
2. Argentina's capital, Buenos Aires, plays a large role in the country's government and economy today.
3. Uruguay has been influenced by its neighbors.
4. Paraguay is the most rural country in the region.

Key Terms and Places

gauchos Argentine cowboys

Buenos Aires capital of Argentina

Mercosur organization that promotes trade and economic cooperation among the southern and eastern countries of South America

informal economy part of the economy based on odd jobs that people perform without government regulation through taxes

landlocked completely surrounded by land with no direct access to the ocean

Lesson Summary
ARGENTINA'S HISTORY AND CULTURE

Argentina was originally home to groups of Indians. In the 1500s Spanish conquerors spread into southern South America in search of silver and gold. They built settlements in Argentina. Spanish monarchs granted land to the colonists. Landowners forced Indians living there to work.

During the colonial era, the Pampas became an important agricultural region. Argentine cowboys, called **gauchos**, herded cattle and horses there.

Argentina gained independence in the 1800s. Many Indians were killed. Immigrants from Italy, Germany, and Spain began to arrive in Argentina.

During the 1970s, many Argentines were tortured and killed after being accused of disagreeing with the government. Argentina's

> **Why did Spanish conquerors come to the region in the 1500s?**
> _____
> _____

> **Immigrants began to arrive from what European countries?**
> _____
> _____

Lesson 3, *continued*

military government gave up power to an elected government in the 1980s. Argentina's historical ties to Europe still affect its culture. Most Argentinians are Roman Catholic.

ARGENTINA TODAY

Buenos Aires is the capital of Argentina. It is the second-largest urban area in South America. In the 1990s, government leaders made economic reforms to help businesses grow. Argentina joined **Mercosur**—an organization that promotes trade and economic cooperation among the southern and eastern countries of South America. However, heavy debt and government spending brought Argentina into an economic crisis. Many people lost their jobs and joined the **informal economy**—a part of the economy based on odd jobs that people perform without government regulation through taxes.

What is the purpose of Mercosur?

_____

_____

_____

_____

URUGUAY

Uruguay lies between Argentina and Brazil. Its capital is Montevideo. Portugal claimed Uruguay during the colonial era, but the Spanish took over in the 1770s. Few Uruguayan Indians remained. Uruguay declared its independence from Spain in 1825. Today Uruguay is a democracy. The economy is based on agriculture and some manufacturing.

What is the capital of Uruguay?

_____

PARAGUAY

Paraguay is **landlocked**, which means completely surrounded by land with no direct access to the ocean. It was claimed by the Spanish in the mid-1530s and remained a Spanish colony until 1811, when it won independence. Today Paraguay is a democracy. Ninety-five percent of Paraguayans are mestizos. People of European descent and Indians make up the rest of the

Underline the definition of landlocked.

What type of government do Uruguay and Paraguay have today?

_____

Guided Reading Workbook

population. Most Paraguayans speak both
Spanish and Guarani, an Indian language.
Agriculture is an important part of the economy.

CHALLENGE ACTIVITY

Critical Thinking: Make Inferences Which
Atlantic South American country do you think
has the strongest economy? Write a paragraph
giving reasons supporting your answer.

DIRECTIONS Read each sentence and fill in the blank with the
word in the word pair that best completes the sentence.

1. Cowboys in Argentina are known as _____.
   (**gauchos/Guarani**)

2. The _____ in Argentina is based on odd jobs performed
   without government regulation through taxes. (**Mercosur/informal economy**)

3. Portugal claimed _____ during the colonial era.
   (**Argentina/Uruguay**)

4. _____ is completely surrounded by land with no direct
   access to the ocean. (**Paraguay/Uruguay**)

5. The capital of Argentina is _____.
   (**Buenos Aires/Montevideo**)

DIRECTIONS Look at each set of four terms following each
number. On the line provided, write the letter of the term that does
not relate to the others.

_____ 6. a. Argentina   b. Montevideo   c. gauchos   d. Buenos Aires

_____ 7. a. trade   b. Mercosur   c. cooperation   d. rural

_____ 8. a. Paraguay   b. Guarani   c. coastal   d. landlocked

_____ 9. a. agriculture b. urban   c. Buenos Aires   d. Uruguay

_____10. a. economy   b. Spanish   c. mestizo   d. Portuguese

Lesson 4

MAIN IDEAS
1. Native cultures, Spanish conquest, and independence shaped Colombia's history.
2. In Colombia today, the benefits of a rich culture and many natural resources contrast with the effects of a long period of civil war.
3. Spanish settlement shaped the history and culture of Venezuela.
4. Oil production plays a large role in Venezuela's economy and government today.
5. The Guianas have diverse cultures and plentiful resources.

Key Terms and Places

Cartagena major Caribbean naval base and port during the Spanish empire

Bogotá capital of Colombia, located high in the eastern Andes

guerrillas members of an irregular military force

Caracas capital of Venezuela and the economic and cultural center of the country

llaneros Venezuelan cowboys

Lake Maracaibo lake near the Caribbean Sea, rich in oil deposits

strike group of workers stopping work until their demands are met

Lesson Summary
COLOMBIA'S HISTORY

In ancient times, the Chibcha people lived in Colombia. They had a well-developed civilization. They made pottery, wove fabrics, and made fine objects from gold and other metals. The Spanish claimed the land, started a colony, and built large estates. They forced the Chibcha and enslaved Africans to work on them. The Spanish also built a large naval base and commercial port at the city of **Cartagena**. Even after independence from Spain, there was trouble in Colombia. Part of the problem is Colombia's rugged geography, which isolates people into separate regions. Many people identify with their region more than their nation.

> Who were the inhabitants of Colombia in ancient times?
> _____

COLOMBIA TODAY

Most Colombians live in the fertile valleys and river basins among the mountain ranges, where the climate is moderate. **Bogotá**, the capital, is located high in the eastern Andes. Each region has a distinct geography as well as a distinct culture. Colombia's major export is oil. Its most famous agricultural product is coffee. Today, **guerrillas** have seized land from farmers and are involved in growing the illegal coca plant, which is used to make the dangerous drug cocaine. Colombia's government continues to fight the guerrillas with laws and military action.

> What is Colombia's most famous agricultural product?
>
> _____

VENEZUELA'S HISTORY

The Spanish came to Venezuela in the early 1500s looking for gold, but found little. In the early 1800s the Venezuelan people, led by Simon Bolívar, revolted against their Spanish rulers and fought for independence, which they officially gained in 1830. Military dictators ran the country throughout the 1800s. Oil was discovered in the 1900s but brought wealth only to the powerful.

> Who led the Venezuelan fight for independence?
>
> _____

VENEZUELA TODAY

Venezuelans are of native Indian, African, and European descent. European descendants tend to live in the cities, and African descendants tend to live on the coast. Most people are Spanish-speaking Roman Catholics, but Indian languages and religious beliefs have been kept alive. **Caracas**, Venezuela's capital, is the country's economic and cultural center. It has modern subways and buildings, but it is surrounded by slums. Many people in rural Venezuela are farmers or ranchers. Cattle on the ranches are herded by **llaneros**, or cowboys of the Llanos. The Orinoco River basin and **Lake Maracaibo** are rich in oil. The oil industry has made some people wealthy, but the vast majority of the population lives in poverty.

> Why do you think there is significant poverty in Venezuela?
>
> _____
>
> _____

After years of military dictators, the first president was elected in 1959. In 2002 President Hugo Chavez started to distribute the country's oil income equally among all Venezuelans. Oil workers went on **strike** to protest the president's actions. The country's economy suffered greatly.

> **How did oil workers protest the actions of President Chavez?**
> _____

THE GUIANAS

The Guianas consist of the countries of Guyana, Suriname, and French Guiana. Dense tropical rain forests cover much of this region. These countries have diverse populations with many people descended from Africans, but each country is different. Guyana has many immigrants from India who came to work on sugarcane plantations. Today most people run small farms or businesses. Suriname's population includes Creoles, or people of mixed heritage, and people from China, Indonesia, Africa, and South Asia. Suriname's economy is similar to Guyana's. French Guiana is a territory of France. Most people live in coastal areas, and the country relies heavily on imports.

> **Circle the names of the countries that make up the Guianas.**

CHALLENGE ACTIVITY

Critical Thinking: Draw Conclusions Did President Hugo Chavez help his country? Write a short paragraph explaining your answer.

Bogotá	Caracas	Cartagena
guerrillas	Lake Maracaibo	llaneros
strike		

DIRECTIONS On the line provided before each statement, write **T** if a statement is true and **F** if a statement is false. If the statement is false, write the term from the word bank that would make the statement correct on the line after each sentence.

_____ 1. The Orinoco River Basin and <u>Lake Maracaibo</u> are particularly rich in oil.

_____

_____ 2. <u>Guyana</u> is the economic center and capital city of Venezuela.

_____

_____ 3. In 2002 oil workers protested their president's control of oil by calling for a <u>strike.</u>

_____

_____ 4. <u>Guerrillas</u> are cowboys who herd cattle on ranches in the Llanos region.

_____

DIRECTIONS Answer each question by writing a sentence that contains at least one term from the word bank.

5. Why is civil war a major problem in Colombia today?

_____

_____

6. What did the Spanish do after conquering the Chibcha culture?

_____

_____

7. Where is Colombia's capital city located?

_____

MAIN IDEAS
1. The countries of Pacific South America share a history influenced by the Inca civilization and Spanish colonization.
2. The culture of Pacific South America includes American Indian and Spanish influences.
3. Ecuador struggles with poverty and political instability.
4. Bolivia's government is trying to gain stability and improve the economy.
5. Peru has made progress against poverty and violence.
6. Chile has a stable government and a strong economy.

Key Terms and Places

viceroy governor of a Spanish colony

Creoles American-born descendants of Europeans

Quito capital of Ecuador

La Paz one of Bolivia's two capital cities

Lima capital of Peru

coup sudden overthrow of a government by a small group of people

Santiago capital of Chile

Lesson Summary
PACIFIC SOUTH AMERICA'S HISTORY

Thousands of years ago, people in Pacific South America learned how to adapt to and modify their environments. They built stone terraces into the steep mountainsides so they could raise crops. In coastal areas, people created irrigation systems to store water and control flooding. Eventually, the Inca Empire came to rule most of the region. They built stone-paved roads and used irrigation to turn the desert into farmland. Their civilization was destroyed by Spanish explorers seeking gold and silver. The Spanish **viceroy**, or governor, made the Indians follow Spanish laws and customs. By the early 1800s people began to revolt against Spanish rule. **Creoles**, American-born descendants of Europeans, were the main

> How did people in Pacific South America farm on rugged land?
>
> _____
>
> _____
>
> _____

leaders. These revolts helped Chile, Ecuador, Bolivia, and Peru gain independence by 1825.

PACIFIC SOUTH AMERICA'S CULTURE

Most people in the region speak Spanish, an official language in every country in the region. However, millions of South American Indians speak a native language. Bolivia, which has the highest percentage of Indians in South America, has three official languages: Spanish and two Indian languages. The religion of this region also reflects both Spanish and native Indian influences. Roman Catholic traditions come from the Spanish, but some people in the Andes still practice ancient religious customs.

> Which country has three official languages?
>
> _____

ECUADOR TODAY

Ecuador has faced recent instability. Widespread poverty is a constant threat to a stable government in this country. Although Ecuador is a democracy, it has not had a stable or popular government for a long time. Ecuador has three economic regions. Most of the agriculture and industry is found along the coastal plain region. The Andes region, where the capital, **Quito**, is located, is poor. Tourism is a major industry there. The third region, the Amazon basin, produces Ecuador's major export, oil.

> Underline the region of Ecuador that has tourism as a major industry.

BOLIVIA TODAY

After many years of military rule, Bolivia is now a democracy. The nation has two capitals. The supreme court meets in Sucre. The congress meets in **La Paz**, the highest capital city in the world. Bolivia is the poorest country in South America, although it does have resources such as metals and natural gas.

> What are Bolivia's two capitals?
>
> _____
>
> _____

PERU TODAY

Peru is the largest and most populous country in Pacific South America. Today it is making some progress against political violence and poverty. Its capital, **Lima**, is the region's largest city. Most poor people build themselves homes on the outskirts of Lima. These settlements are called "young towns." In the 1980s and 1990s, a terrorist group called the Shining Path used violence to oppose the government. After arresting the leaders, the government of Peru has made progress in fighting political violence and poverty. Peru has mineral deposits near the coast, and hydroelectric projects provide energy.

> **What group used violence to oppose the government of Peru?**
> _____
> _____
> _____

CHILE TODAY

Like Peru, Chile has ended a long, violent period. Chile now has a stable government and a growing economy. In the 1970s Chile's elected president was overthrown in a U.S.-backed military **coup**. The military leaders later imprisoned or killed thousands of their political opponents. In the late 1980s, Chileans restored democracy. The economy is now the strongest in the region and poverty rates have decreased. About one-third of Chileans live in central Chile. The capital, **Santiago**, is in this region. This area has a Mediterranean climate good for crops such as grapes used for making wine. Besides farming, fishing, and forestry, Chile's industries include copper mining, which accounts for one-third of Chile's exports. A massive earthquake in 2010 caused major damage in Chile.

> **Underline Chile's industries.**

CHALLENGE ACTIVITY

Critical Thinking: Compare and Contrast You are
a recent arrival to a "young town" in Lima. Write
a letter to a friend in another country about Lima
and your home.

DIRECTIONS Read each sentence and fill in the blank with the
word in the word pair that best completes the sentence.

1. The Spanish appointed _____ to govern its colonies.
    (**Creoles/viceroys**)

2. _____ is the highest capital city in the world. (**La Paz/Quito**)

3. The main leaders in the region's revolt against Spanish rule were
    _____. (**Creoles/Callao**)

4. Chile's capital city, _____, has a mild Mediterranean
    climate. (**Santiago/Valparaíso**)

coup	Creoles	La Paz
Lima	Quito	Santiago
viceroy		

DIRECTIONS Answer each question by writing a sentence that
contains at least one term from the word bank.

5. Where does Bolivia's congress meet?

    _____

    _____

6. How would you describe Ecuador's capital?

    _____

    _____

7. What happened to the president of Chile in the 1970s?

    _____

    _____

Europe before the 1700s

MAIN IDEAS
1. Scientists study the remains of early humans to learn about prehistory.
2. Early humans moved out of Africa and migrated all over the world.
3. People adapted to new environments by making clothing and new types of tools.
4. The first farmers learned to grow plants and raise animals in the New Stone Age.
5. Farming changed societies and the way people lived.

Key Terms and Places

prehistory time before there was writing

tool handheld object that has been modified to help a person accomplish a task

Paleolithic Era first part of the Stone Age

society community of people who share a common culture

hunter-gatherers people who hunt animals and gather wild plants, seeds, fruits, and nuts to survive

migrate move to a new place

ice ages long periods of freezing weather

land bridge strip of land connecting two continents

Mesolithic Era Middle Stone Age

Neolithic Era New Stone Age

domestication process of changing plants or animals to make them more useful to humans

agriculture farming

megaliths huge stones used as monuments or as the sites for religious gatherings

Lesson Summary
PREHISTORIC HUMANS
Prehistory refers to the time before written history. Historians use the work of archaeologists and anthropologists to study prehistory. The first humans and their ancestors lived during an era

How do historians study prehistory?

_____

_____

_____

called the Stone Age. The Stone Age is divided into three periods based on the kinds of **tools** used at the time. The first part of the Stone Age is called the **Paleolithic Era**, or Old Stone Age. During this time people made tools of stone, particularly flint. Flint is easy to shape, and tools made from it can be very sharp. Attaching wooden handles to tools made them more useful.

As early humans developed tools and new hunting techniques, they formed societies. Each **society** developed a culture with language, religion, and art. The early humans of the Stone Age were **hunter-gatherers**. The most important development of early Stone Age culture was language. People also created art by carving stone, ivory, or bone, and by painting images on cave walls. Many scientists think that the first human religions developed during the Stone Age.

> Underline the sentence that lists parts of a culture.

PEOPLE MOVE OUT OF AFRICA

During the Old Stone Age, climate patterns around the world changed, causing people to **migrate**, or move to new places. Many places around the world experienced long periods of freezing weather called **ice ages**. During the ice ages, huge sheets of ice covered much of the earth's land. Scientists think that during the ice ages, the ocean level dropped and exposed a **land bridge** between Asia and North America. Land bridges allowed Stone Age peoples to migrate around the world. Humans migrated from Africa to Asia, Europe, and North America.

> How do scientists think people moved from Asia to North America during the ice ages?
> _____

PEOPLE ADAPT TO NEW ENVIRONMENTS

As early people moved to new lands, they found environments very different from those in East Africa. Many places were much colder and had new plants and animals. Early people had to adapt to these different environments. They learned to make clothing of animal skins and to

> How did early people adapt to different environments?
> _____
> _____
> _____
> _____

make shelters and houses. They also adapted
with new tools, which were smaller and more
complex than tools from the Old Stone Age. This
was the **Mesolithic Era**, or the Middle Stone Age.

THE FIRST FARMERS

The Middle Stone Age was followed by the
Neolithic Era, or New Stone Age. During the
New Stone Age, people learned to polish stones
to make tools like saws and drills. People also
learned how to make fire. Before, they could only
use fire that had been started by natural causes
such as lightning. However, the biggest changes
came in how people produced food. People
learned to plant seed and grow crops. They also
began keeping goats for milk, food, and wool,
and larger animals to carry or pull loads. The
domestication of plants and animals led to the
development of **agriculture**, or farming. For the
first time, people could produce their own food.
This changed human society forever.

> Underline the sentence
> that explains how
> domestication related to
> farming.

FARMING CHANGES SOCIETIES

Domestication of plants and animals allowed
people to look beyond survival. They also began
to build permanent settlements rather than
moving from place to place. They grew enough
food to have a surplus which they could trade.
Societies became more wealthy, and they began
to divide people into classes based on wealth.
People gathered to perform religious ceremonies.
Some put up **megaliths** and honored gods and
goddesses of air, water, fire, earth, and animals.

> How did a surplus of food
> change society?
> _____
> _____
> _____
> _____
> _____

CHALLENGE ACTIVITY

Critical Thinking: Explain Write a paragraph
explaining how the ability to use fire changed life
in the Neolithic Era. In what ways did life
change?

agriculture	domestication	hunger-gatherers
Mesolithic Era	land bridge	megaliths
Paleolithic Era	migrate	Neolithic Era
tool	prehistory	society

DIRECTIONS On the line provided before each statement, write **T** if the statement is true and **F** if the statement is false. If the statement is false, write the correct term from the word bank on the line after each sentence that would make the sentence a true statement.

_____ 1. Historians rely on anthropologists and archaeologists to study <u>history</u>.

_____

_____ 2. Scientists believe that a land bridge formed between Asia and North America during the <u>Neolithic Era</u>.

_____

_____ 3. The <u>domestication</u> of plants and animals led to the development of farming.

_____

_____ 4. People learned to make polished stone saws and drills during the <u>Mesolithic Era</u>.

_____

_____ 5. During the ice ages, people began to <u>migrate</u> around the world.

_____

DIRECTIONS Answer each question by writing a sentence that contains at least two words from the word bank.

6. How did changing climate patterns change the lives of people?

_____

_____

7. How did developing plants and animals for use change life for people?

_____

_____

Europe before the 1700s

Lesson 2

 MAIN IDEAS
1. Early Greek culture saw the rise of the city-state and the creation of colonies.
2. The golden age of Greece saw advances in government, art, and philosophy.
3. Alexander the Great formed a huge empire and spread Greek culture into new areas.

Key Terms and Places

city-states political units made up of a city and all the surrounding lands

golden age period in a society's history marked by great achievements

Athens city-state in eastern Greece

Sparta rival city-state to Athens

Hellenistic Greek-like

Lesson Summary
EARLY GREEK CULTURE

To protect against invaders, early Greeks joined together. Over time, they developed into **city-states**, political units made up of a city and its surrounding lands. In time, some city-states formed colonies, or new cities—and Greek culture spread.

> **What was an effect of city-states forming new colonies?**
> _____
> _____

THE GOLDEN AGE OF GREECE

Greece is famous for its many contributions to world culture, especially during a period of great achievements called the **golden age**. Greece's golden age took place between 500 and 300 BC, after **Athens** and other city-states defeated a powerful Persian army around 500 BC. The defeat of the Persians increased the confidence of the Greeks, and they began to make many advances in art, writing, and thinking.

Athens became the cultural center of Greece during the golden age. Leaders such as Pericles supported the arts and other great works. But these leaders did not rule Athens. The city

> **Briefly define "golden age."**
> _____
> _____

> **Underline the sentence that explains how the defeat of the Persians contributed to the rise of Greece's golden age.**

Guided Reading Workbook

became the world's first democracy. Power was in the hands of the people, who voted in an assembly, which made the laws.

Many accomplishments in art, architecture, literature, philosophy, and science took place during Greece's golden age. Among the earliest Greek writings are two epic poems by Homer. Drama, or plays, became an important part of Greek literature. Greek philosophers such as Socrates, Plato, and Aristotle continue to shape how we think today.

> Underline the areas of accomplishment during the golden age.

Greece's golden age came to an end when Athens and its rival **Sparta** went to war. Sparta had a strong army and was jealous of Athens's influence in Greece. The war raged for years, with other city-states joining in. Sparta finally won, but Greece overall had been weakened. It lay open to a foreign conqueror to take over.

THE EMPIRE OF ALEXANDER

That conqueror was Alexander the Great, who took over Greece in the 330s BC. He conquered not only Greece, but also huge areas of the rest of the world from Greece to India and most of central Asia. He dreamed of conquering more territory, but his tired and homesick troops refused to continue. Alexander died on his return home at the age of 33.

> Do you think Alexander could have taken over Greece if Sparta and Athens had not gone to war? Why or why not?
>
> _____
> _____
> _____

Alexander wanted to spread Greek culture throughout his empire. He urged Greek people to move to new cities. Many Greeks did move. Greek culture then blended with other cultures. These blended cultures are referred to as **Hellenistic**, or Greek-like.

> What was Alexander's attitude toward Greek culture?
>
> _____
> _____

CHALLENGE ACTIVITY

Critical Thinking: Analyze Write a brief article describing Athens from the viewpoint of a writer in Greece's golden age. In your article, include information about the many accomplishments during Greece's golden age.

Athens	city-states	colonies	empire
golden age	Hellenistic	Sparta	

DIRECTIONS On the line provided before each statement, write **T** if the statement is true and **F** if the statement is false. If the statement is false, write the correct term from the word bank on the line after each sentence to make the sentence a true statement.

_____ 1. <u>City-states</u> are political units made up of a city and all the surrounding lands.

_____

_____ 2. A period in a society's history marked by great achievements is called a/an <u>empire</u>.

_____

_____ 3. <u>Sparta</u> was a city-state in eastern Greece that led the fight against the invading Persians around 500 BC.

_____

_____ 4. A Greek-like blended culture is also called <u>Sparta</u>.

_____

_____ 5. Greece was weakened by a war between <u>Alexander the Great</u> and Athens.

_____

Europe before the 1700s

MAIN IDEAS
1. The Roman Republic was governed by elected leaders.
2. The Roman Empire was a time of great achievements.
3. The spread of Christianity began during the empire.
4. Various factors helped bring about the decline of Rome.

Key Terms and Places

Rome city in Italy

republic type of government in which people elect leaders to make laws for them

Senate council of rich and powerful Romans who helped run the city

citizens people who could take part in the Roman government

Carthage city in North Africa

empire land that includes many different peoples and lands under one rule

aqueducts channels used to carry water over long distances

Lesson Summary
THE ROMAN REPUBLIC

Rome began as a small city in Italy. It was ruled by a series of kings, some of whom were cruel rulers. Over time the Romans formed a **republic**, in which elected leaders made all government decisions. The leaders worked with the **Senate**, a group of powerful men. **Citizens** voted and ran for office.

Before long, Rome began to expand its territory. It took over much of the Mediterranean world, including the city of **Carthage** in North Africa. A general named Julius Caesar conquered many new lands. Afraid of his power, a group of senators killed him in 44 BC.

> What is a republic?
>
> _____
> _____
> _____
> _____

THE ROMAN EMPIRE

Caesar's adopted son Octavian became Rome's first emperor, ruling a huge **empire**. This far-flung land contained many different people. Octavian was also called Augustus, or "honored one," because of his many accomplishments. Augustus

> Circle the name of Rome's first emperor.

conquered many new lands. He built monuments
and roads.

The Romans had a long period of peace and
achievement called the Pax Romana. Their many
building projects included **aqueducts**, roads, and
bridges. The Romans also wrote literature and
built a legal system that has had worldwide
influence. The founders of the United States used
the Roman government as a model.

> **In what way does the Roman government affect the United States today?**
>
> _____
> _____
> _____
> _____

THE SPREAD OF CHRISTIANITY

Christianity first appeared in the Roman Empire.
The religion was based on the teachings of Jesus
of Nazareth. Jesus' followers preached
throughout the Roman world. For many years,
Rome tried unsuccessfully to stop the spread of
Christianity. Then in the 300s an emperor named
Constantine became a Christian. Christianity
soon became Rome's official religion. By the end
of the 300s it had become a powerful force in the
Roman world.

> **Underline the name of the Roman emperor who converted to Christianity.**

THE DECLINE OF ROME

Rome's decline had several causes. A number of
bad emperors ignored their duties and the needs
of the Roman people. Military leaders tried to
take over, but many of them were poor rulers as
well. The empire also became too large to control.

The emperor Constantine created a new capital
in a central location. But this change was not
enough. The empire, weakened by its internal
problems, was vulnerable to invaders the Romans
called barbarians. In 476 they attacked Rome and
removed its emperor. The Roman Empire was
no more.

> **Why is the year 476 considered the end of the Roman Empire?**
>
> _____
> _____
> _____
> _____

CHALLENGE ACTIVITY

Critical Thinking: Analyze Write a letter from a
Roman citizen to either Constantine or Augustus,
asking him to take action to improve the Roman
Empire. Include reasons why this action is
needed, based on details in the section.

DIRECTIONS Read each sentence and fill in the blank with the
word in the word pair that best completes the sentence.

1. The city of _____ is thought to have been set up in
   753 BC by a group called the Latins. (**Rome/Carthage**)

2. The _____ was made up of rich and powerful
   Romans who helped run the city. (**Pax Romana/Senate**)

3. _____ were people who could take part in Rome's
   government. (**Citizens/Aqueducts**)

4. A _____ is a form of government that has the people
   vote for leaders to make the laws. (**Senate/republic**)

5. Under Octavian's leadership, Rome became a/an _____, a
   land that included many different peoples under one rule. (**republic/empire**)

6. In addition to roads and bridges, Roman engineers built
   _____, channels used to carry water over long
   distances. (**aqueducts/Pax Romana**)

7. The long period of peace and achievement that Rome experienced is called
   the _____. (**Pax Romana/Colosseum**)

aqueducts	Carthage	citizens	Colosseum
empire	facilitate	Pax Romana	Republic
Rome	Senate		

DIRECTIONS Choose five of the words from the word bank. On a
separate sheet of paper, use these words to write a poem or short
story that relates to the lesson.

Europe before the 1700s

Lesson 4

MAIN IDEAS
1. Eastern emperors ruled from Constantinople and tried but failed to reunite the whole Roman Empire.
2. The people of the eastern empire created a new society that was very different from society in the west.
3. Byzantine Christianity was different from religion in the west.

Key Terms and Places

Constantinople eastern capital of the Roman Empire

Byzantine Empire society that developed in the eastern Roman Empire after the west fell

mosaics pictures made with pieces of colored stone or glass

Lesson Summary
EMPERORS RULE FROM CONSTANTINOPLE

The capital of the eastern Roman Empire was **Constantinople**. The city was located between two seas. It controlled trade between Asia and Europe. After the fall of Rome in 476, this city was the center of Roman power.

The emperor Justinian ruled from 527 to 565. He tried to conquer lands to reunite the old Roman Empire. Justinian made other changes as well. He simplified Roman laws and organized them into a legal system called Justinian's Code. The code helped guarantee fairer treatment for all.

Justinian had many successes, but he also made enemies. These enemies tried to overthrow him in 532. His wife Theodora convinced Justinian to stay in Constantinople and fight. With her advice, he found a way to end the riots.

The eastern empire began to decline after Justinian died. Invaders took away all the land he had gained. Nearly 900 years after Justinian died, the eastern Roman Empire finally ended. In 1453 Ottoman Turks captured Constantinople. With

What was Justinian's Code?
_____
_____

Circle the name of Justinian's wife.

Underline the sentence that explains when and why the Roman Empire ended.

Guided Reading Workbook

this defeat the 1,000-year history of the eastern
Roman Empire came to an end.

A NEW SOCIETY

After Justinian's death, non-Roman influences
took hold throughout the empire. Many people
spoke Greek, and scholars studied Greek
philosophy. A new society developed. This
society is called the **Byzantine Empire**. The
Byzantines interacted with many groups, largely
because of trade.

The eastern empire was different from the
western empire in another way. Byzantine
emperors had more power than western emperors
did. They were the heads of the church as well as
political rulers. The leaders of the church in the
west were bishops and popes. The western
emperors had only political power.

> **What were two ways that the Byzantine Empire was different from the western empire?**
> _____
> _____
> _____
> _____
> _____

BYZANTINE CHRISTIANITY

Christianity was central to the lives of nearly all
Byzantines. Artists created beautiful works of
religious art. Many Byzantine artists made **mosaics**.
These were pictures made with pieces of colored
stone or glass. Some were made of gold, silver, and
jewels. Magnificent churches also were built.

> **Underline the description of mosaics.**

Over time, eastern and western Christianity
became very different. People had different ideas
about how to interpret and practice their religion.
By the 1000s the church split in two. Eastern
Christians formed the Orthodox Church.

CHALLENGE ACTIVITY

Critical Thinking: Compare and Contrast Create a
Venn diagram illustrating the similarities and
differences between the eastern and western
empires. Conduct library or Internet research to
find interesting details for your diagram.

Lesson 4, *continued*

| Byzantine Empire | Constantinople | Hagia Sofia |
| Justinian | mosaics | Theodora |

DIRECTIONS Answer each question by writing a sentence that contains at least one word from the word bank.

1. What city was the capital of the eastern Roman Empire? What was important about this city?

_____

_____

_____

2. Who is considered the last Roman emperor of the eastern empire? What changes occurred after his death?

_____

_____

_____

3. What new society developed in the eastern Roman Empire after the fall of the Roman Empire in the west? Name two ways this new society was different from the Roman Empire in the west.

_____

_____

_____

4. What kind of religious art was popular with Byzantine artists? Describe this type of art.

_____

_____

_____

Europe before the 1700s

MAIN IDEAS
1. The Christian Church influenced nearly every aspect of society in the Middle Ages.
2. Complicated political and economic systems governed life in the Middle Ages.
3. The period after 1000 was a time of great changes in medieval society.

Key Terms and Places

Middle Ages period of history between ancient and modern times that lasted from about 500 until about 1500

pope head of the Roman Catholic Church

Crusade religious war

Holy Land region in which Jesus had lived

Gothic architecture style known for its high pointed ceilings, tall towers, and stained glass windows

feudal system system of exchanging land for military service

manor large estate owned by a noble or a knight

nation-state country united under a single strong government

Lesson Summary
THE CHRISTIAN CHURCH AND SOCIETY

Europe broke into many small kingdoms. The period from about 500 until about 1500 is called the **Middle Ages**. During this time, no one leader could unify Europe, but Christianity tied most Europeans together. As a result, the Christian Church gained influence, and church leaders became powerful.

Circle the dates when the Middle Ages took place.

The **pope** was the head of the Roman Catholic Church. Pope Urban II started a religious war called a **Crusade**. He wanted Europeans to take over the **Holy Land**, where Jesus had lived. It was then ruled by Muslims. The Crusaders failed. However, they brought back new foods, goods, and ideas. Trade between Europe and Asia increased.

Who was the leader of the Roman Catholic Church?
_____

The church had a major influence on art and architecture. Many churches built during this period are examples of **Gothic architecture**. Most people's lives centered around their local church.

LIFE IN THE MIDDLE AGES

Religion was not the only influence on people's lives. Two other major influences were the **feudal system** and the **manor** system.

The feudal system was mainly a relationship between nobles and knights. The nobles gave land to knights. In turn, the knights promised to help defend their lands and the king.

The manor system was a relationship between the owner of the manor and the workers. The owner provided workers with a place to live and a piece of land on which to grow their own food. In exchange, the workers farmed the owner's land.

> **Who participated in the feudal system? In the manor system?**
> _____
> _____
> _____

CHANGES IN MEDIEVAL SOCIETY

France's William the Conqueror invaded England in 1066. He became king and built England's first strong government. In 1215, however, King John of England lost some of his power. A group of nobles drew up a document called Magna Carta, which limited the monarch's power. It gave the nobles power to advise the king.

In 1347 a disease called the Black Death swept through Europe. It killed about a third of the population. The plague caused a labor shortage. As a result, people could demand higher wages.

In 1337 the Hundred Years' War broke out between England and France. The French won, and kings began working to end the feudal system and gain more power. France became a nation-state, a country united under a single government. Other **nation-states** arose around Europe, and the Middle Ages came to an end.

> **How did Magna Carta affect King John?**
> _____

> **What is one negative and one positive outcome of the Black Death?**
> _____
> _____
> _____
> _____
> _____
> _____

CHALLENGE ACTIVITY

Critical Thinking: Make Generalizations Draw up
a document like Magna Carta that includes your
ideas of the basic rights for common people as
well as limits on the power of rulers.

DIRECTIONS Read each sentence and fill in the blank with the
word in the word pair that best completes the sentence.

1. The _____ is the time period between ancient and modern
   times, which lasted from about 500 to 1500. (**Middle Ages/Magna Carta**)

2. The head of the Roman Catholic Church in the Middle Ages was called the
   _____. (**manor/pope**)

3. A religious war is called a _____. (**Crusade/Holy Land**)

4. The pope wanted Europeans to take over the _____, the
   region where Jesus had lived. (**Crusade/Holy Land**)

5. Many churches built in the Middle Ages are examples of
   _____, a style known for its high pointed ceilings, tall towers,
   and stained glass windows. (**feudal system/Gothic architecture**)

6. The system of trading land for military service was called the
   _____. (**feudal system/manor system**)

7. A _____ was a large estate owned by a noble or knight.
   (**peasant/manor**)

8. A _____ was a country that was united under a single strong
   government. (**Holy Land/nation-state**)

Crusade	feudal system	Gothic architecture	Holy Land
Magna Carta	manor	Middle Ages	nation-state
peasant	pope	serf	

DIRECTIONS What would your life be like if you lived in the
Middle Ages? On a separate sheet of paper, write a letter to a friend
and describe what it's like to live in the Middle Ages, using five of
the words in the word bank.

Europe before the 1700s

MAIN IDEAS
1. The Renaissance was a period of new learning, new ideas, and new advances in art, literature, and science.
2. The Reformation changed the religious map of Europe.

Key Terms and Places

Renaissance period of creativity and new ideas that swept Europe from about 1350 through the 1500s

Florence Italian city that became rich through trade during and after the Crusades

Venice Italian city that became rich through trade during and after the Crusades

humanism new way of thinking and learning that emphasized the abilities and accomplishments of human beings

Reformation religious reform movement that began with complaints about problems within the Catholic Church

Protestants Christians who split from the Catholic Church over religious issues

Catholic Reformation series of reforms launched by Catholic Church officials

Lesson Summary
THE RENAISSANCE

The **Renaissance** started in Italy in such cities as **Florence** and **Venice**. These cities became rich through trade. As goods from Asia moved through these cities, Italians became curious about the larger world. At this same time, scholars from other parts of the world came to Italy bringing books written by ancient Greeks and Romans. Interest in Greece and Rome grew. People studied subjects such as history, poetry, and grammar which had been taught in Greek and Roman schools. These subjects are known as the humanities. Increased study of the humanities led to **humanism**—an idea that people are capable of great achievements.

> Circle the name of the country where the Renaissance began.

> Underline three developments that led to the Renaissance.

Renaissance artists developed new painting techniques such as perspective, which made their art look more realistic. The artists Michelangelo and Leonardo da Vinci showed their belief in humanism by making the people in their paintings look like unique individuals. William Shakespeare's plays looked closely at human nature and behavior.

> Circle the names of three Renaissance artists and writers.

Reading about Greek and Roman scientific advances inspired Europeans to study math, astronomy, and other sciences. Some used their new knowledge to create new inventions. Johannes Gutenberg's invention, the movable-type printing press, printed books quickly and cheaply. It spread Renaissance ideas to all parts of Europe.

> What effect did Gutenberg's printing press have on the Renaissance?
> _____
> _____
> _____

THE REFORMATION

The **Reformation**, a religious reform movement, began in Germany. Many people there felt that Catholic Church officials cared more about power than their religious duties. Martin Luther, a German monk, was one of the first people to protest against the church. In 1517 he nailed a list of complaints on a church door in Wittenberg. Angry church officials expelled him from the church. Luther's followers became the first **Protestants**, splitting off from the Catholic Church to form a separate church. Other reformers created their own churches. By 1600 many Europeans had become Protestants.

> Underline the sentence that tells how Luther made his protest.

In response, Catholic Church leaders began a series of reforms, called the **Catholic Reformation**. They asked churches to focus more on religious matters. They tried to make church teachings easier to understand. Priests and teachers went to Asia, Africa, and other lands to spread Catholic teachings. After the Reformation, religious wars broke out in Europe between Catholics and Protestants. These

Lesson 6, *continued*

religious wars led to many changes in Europe.
People began to rely less on church leaders and
look to science for answers.

CHALLENGE ACTIVITY

Critical Thinking: Analyze What events prompted
Catholic leaders to begin the Catholic
Reformation?

Catholic Reformation	Florence	humanism
perspective	Protestants	Reformation
Renaissance	Venice	Wittenberg

DIRECTIONS On the line provided before each statement, write **T** if
a statement is true and **F** if a statement is false. If the statement is
false, write the term from the word bank that would make the
statement correct on the line after each sentence.

_____ 1. Lasting from about 1350 to 1500, the <u>Reformation</u> was a period of
great creativity in Europe.

_____

_____ 2. People who followed Martin Luther in forming their own religion
became the first <u>Protestants</u>.

_____

_____ 3. The technique of <u>humanism</u> enabled artists to show a realistic three-
dimensional scene on a flat surface.

_____

_____ 4. Italian cities such as Florence and <u>Wittenberg</u> became rich through
trade.

_____

_____ 5. <u>Catholic Reformation</u> emphasized the abilities and accomplishments
of human beings.

_____

DIRECTIONS On a separate sheet of paper, write
a story or poem that relates to the lesson. Include
five words from the word bank.

History of Modern Europe

MAIN IDEAS
1. During the Scientific Revolution, discoveries and inventions expanded knowledge and changed life in Europe.
2. In the 1400s and 1500s, Europeans led voyages of discovery and exploration.
3. As Europeans discovered new lands, they created colonies and new empires all over the world.

Key Terms and Places

Scientific Revolution series of events that led to the birth of modern science

New World term used by Europeans to describe the Americas after the voyages of Christopher Columbus

circumnavigate travel all the way around Earth

Columbian Exchange plants, animals, and ideas are exchanged between the New World and the Old World

Lesson Summary
THE SCIENTIFIC REVOLUTION

Before the 1500s most educated people depended on authorities such as ancient Greek writers and church officials for information. During the **Scientific Revolution**, people began to believe that what they observed was more important than what they were told. They developed the scientific method to make logical explanations for how the world worked, based on what they observed. This focus on observation marked the start of modern science.

> Underline the sentence that explains how educated people learned about the world before the Scientific Revolution.

Many Europeans feared the spread of scientific ideas. Church officials opposed many ideas because they went against church teachings. For example, the church taught that the sun circled Earth. From observations using telescopes, scientists now thought that Earth circled the sun. In 1632 church officials arrested Italian scientist Galileo for publishing a book that supported this view. However, science still developed rapidly.

> Why did church officials fear the spread of many scientific ideas?
>
> _____
>
> _____

New discoveries occurred in astronomy, biology, physics, and other fields. New inventions included the telescope, microscope, and thermometer. Isaac Newton made one of the most important discoveries—explaining how gravity works.

THE VOYAGES OF DISCOVERY

With improved devices, such as the compass, astrolabe, and better ships, Europeans made longer, safer sea voyages. They found new routes to distant places. Europeans had many reasons for exploring. Some were curious about the world; some wanted riches, fame, or adventure; and others hoped to spread Christianity. Prince Henry of Portugal sought new trade routes to Asia. After many other voyages, Portuguese explorer Vasco da Gama succeeded in finding a water route to Asia.

The voyages of Christopher Columbus, paid for by Queen Isabella of Spain, were the most significant. His explorations of the **New World** led other European countries to explore this new land, too. Ferdinand Magellan was the first person to attempt to **circumnavigate**, or sail completely around, the world. He was killed, but his crew completed the voyage. Others followed. Voyages of discovery added greatly to European wealth—and people's knowledge of the world.

Circle the three advances that helped make the voyages of discovery possible.

List three explorers and where they explored. _____ _____ _____ _____ _____ _____ _____

NEW EMPIRES

The Spanish were the first Europeans to build colonies in the Americas. Their use of steel swords, firearms, and horses helped them conquer and destroy the Aztec and Inca Empires. Deadly diseases carried by the Spanish also killed many Native Americans. The gold the Spanish found in the Americas made Spain the richest country in Europe. Other European nations also founded colonies in the Americas. In many places

What effect did European explorers and colonists have on Native Americans? _____ _____ _____ _____ _____ _____

Lesson 1, *continued*

they forced out Native Americans. European nations grew rich from trade in wood, fur, and other natural resources.

THE COLUMBIAN EXCHANGE

As Europeans continued to interact with new lands and people, they unexpectedly created a new effect called the **Columbian Exchange**, an exchange of plants, animals, and ideas between the New World and the Old World. As Europeans brought seeds to plant in the Americas, they provided new crops not seen before. They also brought animals, such as horses, and introduced their ideas, religions, language, and technology to the places they conquered. The Europeans also found plants and animals they had never seen before. They took these things back to Europe as well as to Africa and Asia. This exchange of plants changed the eating habits of people around the world.

> **What was the effect created by European explorers between Europe and the Americas?**
> _____
> _____

CHALLENGE ACTIVITY

Critical Thinking: Draw Conclusions Write a paragraph explaining three results of European explorations.

DIRECTIONS Read each sentence and fill in the blank with the word in the word pair that best completes the sentence.

1. In 1632 _____ was arrested for writing that Earth orbited the sun. (**Sir Isaac Newton/Galileo**)

2. The _____ led to the birth of modern science. (**Scientific Revolution/astrolabe**)

3. Without the support of _____, the voyage of Columbus might not have taken place. (**Queen Isabella/Sir Isaac Newton**)

4. In 1498 _____ sailed around the southern tip of Africa and on to Asia. (**Christopher Columbus/Vasco da Gama**)

5. _____ made important observations about the force of gravity. (**Sir Isaac Newton/Galileo**)

DIRECTIONS Write a word or phrase that has the same meaning as the term given.

6. New World _____

7. circumnavigate _____

8. Columbian Exchange_____

_____

9. Scientific Revolution _____

Name _____ Class _____ Date _____

History of Modern Europe

MAIN IDEAS
1. During the Enlightenment, new ideas about government took hold in Europe.
2. The 1600s and 1700s were an Age of Revolution in Europe.
3. Napoleon Bonaparte conquered much of Europe after the French Revolution.

Key Terms

Enlightenment period in the 1600s and 1700s when the use of reason shaped European ideas about society and politics, also known as the Age of Reason

English Bill of Rights 1689 document listing rights of Parliament and the English people

Magna Carta document limiting the power of the English ruler and protecting some rights of the people

Declaration of Independence document signed in 1776 that declared the American colonies' independence from Britain

Declaration of the Rights of Man and of the Citizen French constitution that guaranteed some rights of French citizens and made taxes fairer

Reign of Terror period of great violence during the French Revolution

Lesson Summary
THE ENLIGHTENMENT

During the **Enlightenment** many people questioned common ideas about politics and government. Most of Europe was ruled by kings and queens, also called monarchs. Many monarchs believed God gave them the right to rule as they chose. This belief was called rule by divine right.

Enlightenment thinkers disagreed. John Locke saw government as a contract, or binding legal agreement, between a ruler and the people. A ruler's job was to protect people's rights. If a ruler did not do this, people had the right to change rulers. Jean-Jacques Rousseau also felt government's purpose was to protect people's freedoms. Such ideas inspired revolutions and political change.

> Underline the sentence that explains what rule by divine right is.

> Circle the names of two Enlightenment thinkers who had new ideas about the rights of citizens and the role of government.

Guided Reading Workbook

THE AGE OF REVOLUTION

In the 1600s, England's rulers fought with Parliament for power. As a result, in 1689 Parliament passed the **English Bill of Rights** and made the king agree to honor **Magna Carta**. These steps limited the monarch's power and gave more rights to Parliament and the English people.

> How did the English Bill of Rights and Magna Carta limit the monarch's power?
>
> _____
>
> _____
>
> _____

Enlightenment ideas spread to Britain's North American colonies. There, colonial leaders claimed Britain had denied their rights—and started the American Revolution. In July 1776 Americans signed the **Declaration of Independence**, declaring the American colonies' independence.

The American victory inspired the French people to fight for their rights. Members of the Third Estate, France's largest and poorest social class, demanded a part in government. They formed the National Assembly and demanded that the king limit his powers. When he refused, the French Revolution began. The National Assembly then issued the **Declaration of the Rights of Man and of the Citizen**, a new constitution for France.

> Circle the names of two documents in addition to the English Bill of Rights that changed how rulers governed and that gave citizens more rights.

France's revolutionary leaders ended the monarchy, but soon after the **Reign of Terror** began. It was a very violent time. After it ended, a strong leader rose to power.

NAPOLEON BONAPARTE

In 1799 Napoleon Bonaparte took control of France. He conquered most of Europe and built a French empire. Napoleon created a fairer legal system, called the Napoleonic Code, but he was a harsh ruler. Napoleon's armies were defeated in 1814 and 1815. Soon after, European leaders redrew the map of Europe to prevent any other country from becoming too powerful.

> List two of Napoleon's achievements.
>
> _____
>
> _____
>
> _____
>
> _____
>
> _____

CHALLENGE ACTIVITY

Critical Thinking: Draw Conclusions In the Age
of Revolution, were ideas or armies more
important? Give support for your answer.

Declaration of Independence	Declaration of the Rights of Man and of the Citizen
English Bill of Rights	Enlightenment
Magna Carta	Reign of Terror

DIRECTIONS Answer each question by writing a sentence that
contains at least one term from the word bank.

1. How did England's Parliament limit the monarchy's power?

   _____

   _____

2. What peaceful steps did France take to guarantee its people more freedoms?

   _____

   _____

3. What effect did Enlightenment ideas have on the British colonies in North America?

   _____

   _____

4. What period came right after the French Revolution? Why was it called this?

   _____

   _____

5. What was the Age of Reason?

   _____

   _____

History of Modern Europe

MAIN IDEAS
1. Britain's large labor force, raw materials, and money to invest led to the start of the Industrial Revolution.
2. Industrial growth began in Great Britain and then spread to other parts of Europe.
3. The Industrial Revolution led to both positive and negative changes in society.

Key Terms

Industrial Revolution period of rapid growth in machine-made goods

textiles cloth products

capitalism economic system in which individuals own most businesses and resources, and people invest money in hopes of making a profit

suffragettes women who campaigned for the right to vote

Lesson Summary
START OF THE INDUSTRIAL REVOLUTION

Changes in agriculture helped prepare Britain for industrial growth. Rich farmers bought land and created larger, more efficient farms. At the same time, Europe's population grew, creating a need for more food. To meet this need, farmers tried new farming methods and invented new machines.

> Underline the sentence that tells why farmers needed to grow more food.

These improved methods and inventions helped farmers grow more crops, but with fewer workers. As a result, many small farmers and farm workers lost their farms and jobs—and moved to the cities.

In Britain, all these changes sparked the **Industrial Revolution**. By the 1700s, Britain had labor, natural resources, and money to invest—all the resources needed for industry to grow. Demand for manufactured goods soon grew. People looked for ways to make these goods even faster.

> Circle three resources needed for industrial growth.

INDUSTRIAL GROWTH

The **textile** industry, which made cloth products, developed first. In the early 1700s, cloth was made by hand. This began to change in 1769 when Richard Arkwright invented a water-powered spinning machine. Other new machines enabled workers to make large amounts of cloth quickly. As a result, the price of cloth fell. Soon workers were using machines to make other kinds of goods faster and cheaper.

Most early machines relied on water power. Factories, the buildings that housed the machines, had to be built near rivers. In the 1760s James Watt built the first modern steam engine. Factories could now be set up in cities. In 1855 Henry Bessemer invented a new way to make steel, and the steel industry grew. Transportation became faster as steam engines powered boats and trains. Advancements in communication and transportation helped spread ideas and culture more quickly.

Industrial growth changed how people worked. Many people—including children and young women—worked in unsafe factories. They worked long hours, usually for poor wages. However, by the late 1800s, the Industrial Revolution had spread. Industrial growth resulted in a new economic system—**capitalism**, in which individuals own most businesses and resources.

> **Circle the industry that developed first. Then underline the invention that helped it grow fast.**

> **Why do you think the price of cloth fell as workers made more cloth?**
> _____
> _____
> _____

> **Explain why you think the Industrial Revolution led to a new economic system.**
> _____
> _____
> _____

CHANGES IN SOCIETY

The Industrial Revolution made life better for some, but worse for others. Manufactured goods became cheaper. New inventions made life easier. More people joined the middle class. Meanwhile, cities grew, becoming dirty, noisy, and crowded. Workers often remained poor, living in unsafe apartments where diseases spread. Reformers worked to improve society, pushing for safer

> **Underline the sentences that explain how people's lives improved as a result of the Industrial Revolution.**

working conditions, higher wages, and cleaner
cities. Some women, called **suffragettes**, pressed
for the right to vote.

CHALLENGE ACTIVITY

Critical Thinking: Draw Conclusions Did the
benefits of the Industrial Revolution outweigh
the problems it caused? Write a paragraph to
explain your reasons.

DIRECTIONS Look at each set of four terms following each
number. On the line provided, write the letter of the term that does
not relate to the others.

_____ 1. a. voting
      b. suffragette
      c. guillotine
      d. women

_____ 2. a. Henry Bessemer
      b. textiles
      c. cloth
      d. spinning machine

_____ 3. a. capitalism
      b. profit
      c. investment
      d. military

_____ 4. a. inventions
      b. machines
      c. literature
      d. technology

_____ 5. a. steam power
      b. iron
      c. profit
      d. steel

DIRECTIONS Write three words or phrases that describe each term.

6. capitalism _____

_____

7. textiles _____

_____

8. suffragette _____

_____

9. Industrial Revolution _____

_____

Lesson 4

> **MAIN IDEAS**
> 1. Rivalries in Europe led to the outbreak of World War I.
> 2. After a long, devastating war, the Allies claimed victory.
> 3. The war's end brought great political and territorial changes to Europe.

Key Terms

nationalism devotion and loyalty to one's country

imperialism European nations' quest for colonies in Africa and Asia

alliance agreement between countries

trench warfare style of fighting in which each side fights from deep ditches, or trenches, dug into the ground

Treaty of Versailles final peace settlement of World War I

communism political system in which the government owns and controls all aspects of life in a country

Lesson Summary

THE OUTBREAK OF WAR

In the 1800s many people who were ruled by empires wanted to form their own nations. As **nationalism**—devotion and loyalty to one's country—became more common, tensions grew. **Imperialism** also helped set the stage for war. As European countries competed for overseas empires, their rivalry and mistrust deepened. In 1882 Italy, Germany, and Austria-Hungary formed the Triple Alliance. This **alliance** was an agreement to fight together if any of the three was attacked. Britain, Russia, and France also formed an alliance, the Triple Entente. By the 1900s many countries were preparing for war by building up their armies and stockpiling weapons. Germany and Great Britain built strong navies and powerful new battleships.

One source of tension was Bosnia and Herzegovina, a province of Austria-Hungary that neighboring Serbia wanted to control. On June 28,

> Underline the sentence that explains what an alliance is.

> When was Archduke Franz Ferdinand killed?
> _____

Guided Reading Workbook

1914, Archduke Franz Ferdinand of Austria-Hungary was assassinated by a Serbian gunman. Faced with war, Serbia turned to Russia for help. The alliance system split Europe into warring sides.

WAR AND VICTORY

Germany attacked the Allies (France, Great Britain, Serbia, and Russia), sending its army into Belgium and France. Russia attacked the Central Powers (Germany and Austria-Hungary) from the east. The two sides quickly prepared for **trench warfare** by digging hundreds of miles of trenches, which were easy to defend but hard to attack. Millions of soldiers died in the trenches, but neither side could win the war. New weapons, such as machine guns, poison gas, and tanks, were designed to gain an advantage on the battlefield.

> Circle the names of two countries that were part of the Central Powers.

In 1917 German U-boats attacked American ships that were helping Britain. The United States entered the war, strengthening the Allies. Around the same time, Russia pulled out of the war. Germany renewed its attack on the Allies. However, this last effort failed, and the Central Powers surrendered in 1918.

> Why did the United States enter the war?
>
> _____
> _____
> _____

THE WAR'S END

World War I, in which over 8.5 million soldiers died, changed Europe forever. American president Woodrow Wilson wanted a just peace after the war, but the **Treaty of Versailles** blamed Germany alone. The Germans were forced to slash the size of their army, give up overseas colonies, and pay billions of dollars for damages. The German empire gave way to a fragile republic. In Russia, a revolution had established a Communist government. **Communism** is a political system in which the government owns and controls every aspect of life. Austria and Hungary became separate countries, Poland and

> Where was the first Communist government established?
>
> _____

Czechoslovakia gained independence, Yugoslavia
was formed, and Finland, Latvia, Lithuania, and
Estonia broke away from Russia.

CHALLENGE ACTIVITY

Critical Thinking: Draw Inferences Write a
sentence explaining why machine guns and trench
warfare were such a deadly combination.

alliance	Allies	Central Powers	communism
nationalism	Treaty of Versailles	trench warfare	imperialism

DIRECTIONS Answer each question by writing a sentence that
contains at least one term from the word bank.

1. What led to the tension that sparked World War I?

   _____

   _____

2. What countries fought each other in World War I?

   _____

   _____

   _____

3. How did the new kind of fighting seen in World War I affect the soldiers?

   _____

   _____

4. What did the final peace settlement of World War I demand of Germany?

   _____

   _____

   _____

5. How did World War I change the way some European countries were governed?

_____

DIRECTIONS Imagine that you are a newspaper reporter visiting Europe during World War I. On a separate sheet of paper, write a short article that explains what you have learned about the war and the fighting. Include at least five terms from the word bank.

_____

_____

History of Modern Europe

MAIN IDEAS
1. Economic and political problems troubled Europe in the years after World War I.
2. World War II broke out when Germany invaded Poland.
3. Nazi Germany targeted the Jews during the Holocaust.
4. Allied victories in Europe and Japan brought the end of World War II.

Key Terms

Great Depression global economic crisis in the 1930s

dictator ruler who has total control

Axis Powers alliance among Germany, Italy, and Japan

Allies France, Great Britain, and other countries that opposed the Axis

Holocaust attempt by the Nazi government during World War II to eliminate Europe's Jews

Lesson Summary
PROBLEMS TROUBLE EUROPE

With its economy booming after World War I, the United States provided loans to help Europe rebuild. But the U.S. stock market crashed in 1929, starting a global economic crisis, the **Great Depression**. Without United States funds, banks failed in Europe, and many people lost their jobs.

People blamed their leaders for the hard times. In some countries, **dictators** gained power by making false promises. In the 1920s Benito Mussolini spoke of bringing back the glory of the Roman Empire to Italy. Instead he took away people's rights. In Russia in 1924, Joseph Stalin became dictator and oppressed the people, using secret police to spy on them. Promising to restore Germany's military and economic strength, Adolf Hitler rose to power in 1933. Once in power, he outlawed all political parties except the Nazi Party. He also discriminated against Jews and other groups he believed to be inferior.

> What caused many Europeans to lose their jobs after 1929?
>
> _____
> _____
> _____

> Underline the sentence that tells Adolf Hitler's actions when he first took power.

WAR BREAKS OUT

No one moved to stop Mussolini when he invaded Ethiopia in 1935. Meanwhile, Hitler added Austria to the German empire in 1938 and Czechoslovakia in 1939. When Hitler invaded Poland in 1939, France and Britain declared war on Germany, beginning World War II. Germany, Italy, and Japan formed the **Axis Powers**. They were opposed by the **Allies**—France, Great Britain, and others. The Axis won most of the early battles and soon defeated France. Britain withstood intense bombing and did not surrender. The German army then turned toward Eastern Europe and the Soviet Union. Italy invaded North Africa. In 1941 Japan attacked the United States at Pearl Harbor, Hawaii.

> Underline the countries that Mussolini and Hitler invaded.

> Who won most of the early battles in World War II?
> _____

THE HOLOCAUST

The **Holocaust** was the Nazi Party's plan to eliminate people they believed were inferior, especially the Jews. By 1942 the Nazis had put millions of Jews in concentration camps, such as Auschwitz in Poland. Some Jews tried to hide, escape, or fight back. In the end, however, the Nazis killed about two-thirds of Europe's Jews and several million non-Jews.

END OF THE WAR

In 1943 the Allies won key battles. On D-Day in 1944, they invaded Normandy, France, and paved the way for an advance toward Germany. The war ended in 1945 soon after the U.S. dropped an atomic bomb on Japan. The war took the lives of more than 50 million people and led to the formation of the United Nations. The United States helped many countries rebuild. However, the United States and the Soviet Union soon became rivals for power.

> Circle the names of the countries that became rivals for power after World War II.

CHALLENGE ACTIVITY

Critical Thinking: Sequence Make a timeline showing the main events leading up to Germany's invasion of Poland in 1939.

DIRECTIONS On the line provided before each statement, write **T** if the statement is true and **F** if the statement is false. If the statement is false, write the term that makes the sentence a true statement on the line after each sentence.

_____ 1. The two alliances fighting in World War II were the Allies and the <u>Nazi Powers</u>.

_____

_____ 2. The <u>Great Depression</u> was triggered by the stock market crash in 1929.

_____

_____ 3. Benito Mussolini was Italy's first <u>Communist</u>.

_____

_____ 4. During the Holocaust, the <u>Nazi</u> government tried to wipe out Europe's Jews.

_____

_____ 5. <u>Joseph Stalin</u> was the Communist leader of the Soviet Union.

_____

_____ 6. A major victory for the <u>Axis Powers</u> occurred in the D-Day invasion on the beaches of Normandy, France.

_____

Allies	Axis Powers	dictator
Great Depression	Holocaust	Nazi

DIRECTIONS Look up three of the vocabulary terms in the word bank. On a separate sheet of paper, write the dictionary definition of the word that is closest to the definition used in your textbook.

_____

History of Modern Europe

MAIN IDEAS
1. The Cold War divided Europe between democratic and Communist nations.
2. Many Eastern European countries changed boundaries and forms of government at the end of the Cold War.
3. European cooperation has brought economic and political change to Europe.

Key Terms

superpowers strong and influential countries

Cold War period of tense rivalry between the United States and the Soviet Union

arms race competition between countries to build superior weapons

common market group of nations that cooperate to make trade among members easier

European Union (EU) organization that promotes political and economic cooperation in Europe

refugee someone forced to flee his or her own country because of persecution, war, or violence

asylum protection given by a government to someone who has left another country in order to escape being harmed

migrant person who goes from one place to another, especially to find work

Lesson Summary
THE COLD WAR

After World War II, the two **superpowers**—the United States and the Soviet Union—distrusted each other. This led to the **Cold War**, a period of tense rivalry between these two countries. The Soviet Union stood for communism, and the United States stood for democracy and free enterprise.

> Underline the sentence that defines the Cold War.

The United States and several Western nations formed an alliance called the North Atlantic Treaty Organization (NATO). The Soviet Union and most Eastern European countries were allies under the Warsaw Pact. The two sides used the threat of nuclear war to defend themselves.

> Which alliance did most Eastern European countries join after World War II?
>
> _____

Lesson 6, *continued*

Germany was split into East Germany and West Germany. Communist leaders built the Berlin Wall to prevent East Germans from fleeing to the West. Western countries were more successful economically than Communist Eastern Europe. People in the East suffered from shortages of money, food, clothing, and cars.

THE END OF THE COLD WAR

By the 1980s the **arms race**—a competition to build superior weapons—between the Soviet Union and the U.S. was damaging the Soviet economy. To solve the problem, Soviet leader Mikhail Gorbachev made changes. He reduced government control of the economy and held democratic elections.

These policies helped inspire change throughout Eastern Europe. Poland and Czechoslovakia threw off Communist rule. The Berlin Wall came down in 1989. East and West Germany reunited to form a single country again in 1990. In December 1991 the Soviet Union broke up.

> In what year did the Soviet Union break up?
>
> _____

Ukraine, Lithuania, and Belarus became independent countries. In 1993 Czechoslovakia split peacefully into the Czech Republic and Slovakia. However, ethnic conflict in Yugoslavia caused much violence. By 1994 Yugoslavia had split into five countries—Bosnia and Herzegovina, Croatia, Macedonia, Slovenia, and Serbia and Montenegro.

> Underline the five countries that were created when Yugoslavia split.

EUROPEAN COOPERATION

After two deadly wars, many Europeans thought a sense of community would make more wars less likely. In the 1950s West Germany, Luxembourg, Italy, Belgium, France, and the Netherlands moved toward unity with a **common market**, a single economic unit to improve trade among members. Today, 28 countries make up the **European Union (EU)**. Many use a common currency, the euro. The European Union deals with issues such as environment, trade, and migration. Their governing body has executive, legislative, and judicial branches. Representatives are selected from all member nations. The EU has helped unify Europe, and other countries hope to join in the future.

> **Circle the issues that concern the European Union.**

The EU has experienced some turmoil in recent times because some members disagree with specific policies. For example, civil wars in other countries such as Syria have created a **refugee** crisis. Many refugees flee their home countries seeking **asylum**, or protection, in Europe to start new lives. Others, called **migrants**, have fled violence and poverty in Africa, the Middle East, and other regions. European countries struggled to figure out what to do with their new arrivals. This crisis caused divisions in the EU about how to best resettle so many people. These divisions created a new spirit of nationalism in Europe. As a result, the United Kingdom voted to leave the European Union in June 2016. This is the first time a member country has decided to leave the EU.

> **Circle the word that helps to define the meaning of asylum.**

CHALLENGE ACTIVITY

Critical Thinking: Cause and Effect Write a sentence that explains how the establishment of the European Union might make wars in Europe less likely in the future.

DIRECTIONS Read each sentence and fill in the blank with the word in the word pair that best completes the sentence.

1. The United States and the Soviet Union were rivals in the

   _____. **(Cold War/European Union)**

2. The _____ of East and West Germany came in 1989 when the Berlin Wall was torn down. **(common market/reunification)**

3. After the Cold War, _____ led to the breakup of Yugoslavia. **(superpowers/ethnic tensions)**

4. Belgium, France, Italy, Luxembourg, the Netherlands, and West Germany were the first countries to form a common market, which is now known as

   the _____. **(superpowers/European Union)**

5. The high costs of the _____ hurt the Soviet economy. **(arms race/Berlin Wall)**

6. The crisis in Syria has created many _____ seeking asylum. **(migrants/refugees)**

arms race	asylum	Berlin Wall
Cold War	common market	ethnic tensions
European Union (EU)	migrant	refugee
reunification	superpowers	

DIRECTIONS Choose five of the vocabulary words from the word bank. On a separate sheet of paper, use these terms to write a summary of what you learned in the lesson.

_____

_____

_____

Southern Europe

MAIN IDEAS
1. Southern Europe's physical features include rugged mountains and narrow coastal plains.
2. The region's climate and resources support such industries as agriculture, fishing, and tourism.

Key Terms and Places

Mediterranean Sea sea that borders Southern Europe

Pyrenees mountain range separating Spain and France

Apennines mountain range running along the whole Italian Peninsula

Alps Europe's highest mountains, some of which are located in northern Italy

Mediterranean climate type of climate found across Southern Europe, with warm, sunny days and mild nights for most of the year

Lesson Summary
PHYSICAL FEATURES

Southern Europe is composed of three peninsulas—the Iberian, the Italian, and the Balkan—and some large islands. All of the peninsulas have coastlines on the **Mediterranean Sea**.

These peninsulas are largely covered with rugged mountains. The land is so rugged that farming and travel in Southern Europe can be difficult. The **Pyrenees** form a boundary between Spain and France. The **Apennines** run along the Italian Peninsula. The **Alps**—Europe's highest mountains—are in the north. The Pindus Mountains cover much of Greece. The region also has coastal plains and river valleys, where most of the farming is done and where most of the people live. Crete, which is south of Greece, and Sicily, at the southern tip of Italy, are two of the larger islands in the region. Many of the region's islands are the peaks of undersea mountains.

> **What are the three peninsulas of Southern Europe?**
>
> _____
>
> _____
>
> _____

> **Circle the four mountain ranges in Southern Europe.**

Guided Reading Workbook

In addition to the Mediterranean Sea, the Adriatic, Aegean, and Ionian seas are important to Southern Europe. They give the people food and an easy way to travel around the region. The Po and the Tagus are two important rivers in Southern Europe. The Po flows across northern Italy. The Tagus, the region's longest river, flows across the Iberian Peninsula.

> Circle the names of the four seas in Southern Europe.

CLIMATE AND RESOURCES

The climate in Southern Europe is called a **Mediterranean climate**. The climate is warm and sunny in the summer and mild and rainy in the winter. Southern Europe's climate is one of its most valuable resources. It supports the growing of many crops, including citrus fruits, grapes, olives, and wheat. It also attracts millions of tourists each year.

> What are the characteristics of a Mediterranean climate?
> _____
> _____
> _____

The seas are another important resource in Southern Europe. Many of the region's cities are ports, shipping goods all over the world. In addition, the seas support profitable fishing industries.

> Underline two ways in which the seas are a key resource in Southern Europe.

CHALLENGE ACTIVITY

Critical Thinking: Analyze Write a paragraph explaining how Southern Europe's climate supports the region's economy.

| Alps | Apennines | Mediterranean climate |
| Mediterranean Sea | plains | Pyrenees |

DIRECTIONS On the line provided before each statement, write **T** if
a statement is true and **F** if a statement is false. If the statement is
false, write the term from the word bank that would make the
statement true on the line after each sentence.

_____ 1. The <u>Alps</u> form a boundary between Spain and France.

_____

_____ 2. Islands and <u>peninsulas</u> form the region of Southern Europe.

_____

_____ 3. The <u>Apennines</u> are Europe's highest mountain range.

_____

_____ 4. The countries of Southern Europe all share a common location on the
<u>Adriatic Sea</u>.

_____

_____ 5. The <u>Pyrenees</u> run along the Italian Peninsula.

_____

DIRECTIONS Read each sentence and fill in the blank with the
word in the word pair that best completes the sentence.

6. Many of Southern Europe's islands are formed by _____ .

   (undersea mountains/plains)

7. The _____ is ideal for growing a variety of crops.

   (Mediterranean Sea/Mediterranean climate)

Southern Europe

MAIN IDEAS
1. Early in its history, Greece was the home of a great civilization, but it was later ruled by foreign powers.
2. The Greek language, the Orthodox Church, and varied customs have helped shape Greece's culture.
3. In Greece today, many people are looking for new economic opportunities.
4. Italian history can be divided into three periods: ancient Rome, the Renaissance, and unified Italy.
5. Religion and local traditions have helped shape Italy's culture.
6. Italy today has two distinct economic regions—northern Italy and southern Italy.

Key Terms and Places

Orthodox Church branch of Christianity that dates to the Byzantine Empire

Christianity major world religion based on the life and teachings of Jesus of Nazareth

Athens Greece's capital and largest city

Catholicism largest branch of Christianity

pope spiritual head of the Roman Catholic Church

Vatican City independent state within the city of Rome

Sicily island at Italy's southern tip

Naples largest city in southern Italy and an important port

Milan major industrial city in northern Italy and a fashion center

Rome capital of Italy

Lesson Summary
GREECE'S HISTORY

Ancient Greeks are known for their beautiful art, new forms of history and drama, and advances in geometry. They developed a system of reason that is the basis for modern science, and they created democracy. In the 300s BC Greece was conquered by Alexander the Great and was later ruled by the Romans and the Ottoman Turks. In the 1800s Greece became a monarchy. A military dictatorship ruled from 1967 to 1974. More recently, Greece has returned to democracy.

Name two achievements of ancient Greece.
_____
_____
_____
_____
_____
_____

GREECE'S CULTURE

The Greek people today speak a form of the same language spoken by their ancestors. Nearly everyone in Greece is a member of the **Orthodox Church**, a branch of **Christianity** dating from the Byzantine Empire. Religion is important to the Greek people, and religious holidays are popular times for celebration and family gatherings. For centuries, the family has been central to Greek culture, and today it remains the cornerstone of Greek society.

> What is the cornerstone of Greek society?
> _____

GREECE TODAY

About three-fifths of all people in Greece live in cities. **Athens** is the largest city in Greece and is its capital. The city's industry has produced air pollution that damages the ancient ruins and endangers people's health. People in rural areas live much like they did in the past. They grow crops, raise sheep and goats, and socialize in the village square. Greece's economic growth lags behind most other European nations. Greece is a leading country in the shipping industry, with one of the largest shipping fleets in the world. Another profitable industry is tourism.

> Underline two important industries in Greece.

ITALY'S HISTORY

Ancient Rome grew into an empire that stretched from Britain to the Persian Gulf. Ancient Rome's achievements in art, architecture, literature, law, and government still influence the world today. When the Roman Empire collapsed in the AD 400s, cities in Italy formed their own states. Many cities became centers of trade. Wealthy Italian merchants helped bring about the Renaissance through their support of the work of artists and architects. In the mid-1800s a rise in nationalism led to Italian unification in 1861. In the 1920s Italy became a dictatorship under Benito Mussolini. This lasted until Italy's defeat in

> Underline five areas in which the achievements of ancient Rome still influence the world today.

World War II, after which Italy became a
democracy.

ITALY'S CULTURE

Catholicism has historically been the strongest
influence on Italian culture. The **pope** heads the
government of **Vatican City** and the Roman
Catholic Church. Religious holidays and festivals
are major events. Local traditions and regional
geography have also influenced Italian culture.
Italian food varies widely from region to region.
Italians have long been trendsetters in
contemporary art forms, including painting,
composing, fashion, and film.

> **Underline three influences on Italian culture.**

ITALY TODAY

Southern Italy is poorer than northern Italy. It
has less industry and relies on agriculture and
tourism for its survival. Farming is especially
important in **Sicily**. **Naples** is a busy port and an
industrial center. Northern Italy has a strong
economy, including major industrial centers, the
most productive farmland, and the most popular
tourist destinations. **Milan** is an industrial center
and a worldwide center for fashion design. Turin
and Genoa are also industrial centers. Florence,
Pisa, and Venice are popular tourist destinations.
Rome, Italy's capital, is located between northern
Italy and southern Italy.

> **Why is the economy of northern Italy strong?**
>
> _____
> _____
> _____

CHALLENGE ACTIVITY

Critical Thinking: Synthesize Write a sentence to explain how religion and family work together to form a central part of Greek culture.

Athens	Catholicism	Christianity
Milan	Naples	Orthodox Church
pope	Rome	Sicily
Vatican City		

DIRECTIONS Read each sentence and fill in the blank with the word from the word bank that best completes the sentence.

1. Greece's capital and largest city, _____ , has a serious

   air pollution problem.

2. Most people in Greece are members of the _____ .

3. The pope heads the government of _____ , an indepen-

   dent state located within Rome.

4. The _____ is the head of the Roman Catholic Church.

5. The city of _____ in northern Italy is a worldwide

   center for fashion design.

DIRECTIONS Choose five words from the word bank. On a separate sheet of paper, use these words to write a poem, story, or letter that relates to the lesson.

_____

_____

Southern Europe

Lesson 3

MAIN IDEAS

1. Over the centuries, Spain and Portugal have been part of many large and powerful empires.
2. The cultures of Spain and Portugal reflect their long histories.
3. Having been both rich and poor in the past, Spain and Portugal today have struggling economies.

Key Terms and Places

Iberia westernmost peninsula in Europe

parliamentary monarchy form of government in which a king rules with the help of an elected parliament

Madrid capital of Spain

Barcelona center of industry, culture, and tourism in Spain

Lisbon large city in Portugal and important industrial center

Lesson Summary
HISTORY

Spain and Portugal lie on the Iberian Peninsula, or **Iberia**. Both countries have been part of large, powerful empires. Coastal areas of what is now Spain were first ruled by Phoenicians from the eastern Mediterranean. Later the Greeks established colonies there. A few centuries later, Iberia became part of the Roman Empire. After the fall of Rome, Iberia was conquered by the Moors—Muslims from North Africa. For about 600 years, much of the Iberian Peninsula was under Muslim rule.

Eventually the Christian kingdoms of Spain and Portugal banded together to drive out the Muslims and other non-Christians. Both countries went on to establish empires of their own in the Americas, Africa, and Asia. Both countries became rich and powerful until most of their colonies broke away and became independent in the 1800s and 1900s.

> **What foreign powers have ruled Spain and Portugal?**
> _____
> _____

> **Where did Spain and Portugal establish colonies?**
> _____
> _____

Guided Reading Workbook

CULTURE

Many dialects of Spanish and Portuguese are spoken in Iberia. Catalan, which is similar to Spanish, is spoken in eastern Spain. Galician, which is more closely related to Portuguese, is spoken in northwest Spain. The Basques of the Pyrenees have their own language and customs. For this reason, many Basques want independence from Spain. In both Spain and Portugal, the people are mainly Roman Catholic.

Music is important to both countries. The Portuguese are famous for sad folk songs called fados. The Spanish are known for a style of song and dance called flamenco. Much of the peninsula's art and architecture reflect its Muslim past. The round arches and elaborate tilework on many buildings were influenced by Muslim design.

> Circle the group in Spain that has its own language and customs.

> What Muslim influences can be seen on buildings in Iberia?
>
> _____
>
> _____

SPAIN AND PORTUGAL TODAY

When other countries started building industrial economies, Spain and Portugal relied on the wealth from their colonies. When their colonies broke away, the income they had depended on was lost. Despite recent economic growth and strong industries such as tourism, their economies are struggling.

Spain is governed by a **parliamentary monarchy**—a king rules with the help of an elected parliament. **Madrid**—the capital—and **Barcelona** are centers of industry, culture, and tourism.

Portugal is a republic whose leaders are elected. The economy is based on industries in **Lisbon** and other large cities. In rural areas, farmers grow many crops but are most famous for grapes and cork.

> Underline the definition of a parliamentary monarchy.

CHALLENGE ACTIVITY
Critical Thinking: Compare and Contrast
Compare and contrast Spain and Portugal. Then
explain which country you would prefer to visit.

Barcelona	Iberia	Lisbon
Madrid	parliamentary monarchy	

DIRECTIONS Answer each question by writing a sentence that
contains at least one word from the word bank.

1. Describe the geographic setting of Spain and Portugal.

_____

_____

2. How are Spain and Portugal governed today?

_____

_____

3. Where are the centers of industry, tourism, and culture in Spain?

_____

4. Where are the industries of Portugal based?

_____

DIRECTIONS Look at each set of terms. On the line provided, write
the letter of the term that does not relate to the others.

_____ 5. a. Basque   b. Catalan   c. Galician   d. Lisbon

_____ 6. a. Muslim   b. Greek   c. Roman   d. Portuguese

MAIN IDEAS
1. West-Central Europe includes many types of physical features and a mild climate that supports agriculture, energy production, and tourism.
2. Northern Europe contains low mountains, jagged coastlines, a variety of natural resources, and a range of climates.

Key Terms and Places

Northern European Plain broad coastal plain that stretches from the Atlantic coast into Eastern Europe

North Sea large body of water to the north of the region

English Channel narrow waterway to the north of the region that separates West-Central Europe from the United Kingdom

Danube River one of the major rivers of the region

Rhine River one of the major rivers of the region

navigable river river that is deep and wide enough for ships to use

North Atlantic Drift ocean current that brings warm, moist air across the Atlantic Ocean

British Isles group of islands located across the English Channel from the rest of Europe

Scandinavia region of islands and peninsulas in far northern Europe

fjord narrow inlet of the sea set between high, rocky cliffs

geothermal energy energy from the heat of Earth's interior

Lesson Summary
WEST-CENTRAL EUROPE

West-Central Europe has plains, uplands, and mountains. Most of the **Northern European Plain** is flat or rolling. The plain has the region's best farmland and largest cities. The Central Uplands are in the middle of the region. This area has many rounded hills, small plateaus, and valleys. Coal fields have helped to make it a major mining and industrial area. The area is mostly too rocky for farming.

> Circle the three major landform types in West-Central Europe.

The Alps and Pyrenees form the alpine mountain system. The Alps are the highest mountains in Europe. The **North Sea** and the **English Channel** lie to the north. The **Danube River** and the **Rhine River** are important waterways for trade and travel. The region has several **navigable rivers**. These rivers and a system of canals link the region's interior to the seas.

A warm ocean current, the **North Atlantic Drift**, brings warm, moist air across the Atlantic Ocean and creates a marine west coast climate in most of West-Central Europe. Summers are mild, but winters can be cold. In the Alps and other higher elevation areas, the climate is colder and wetter. The mild Mediterranean climate of southern France is a valuable resource. Farmers in this region grow grapes, grains, and vegetables. In the Alps and the uplands, farmers raise livestock. Energy resources are not evenly divided. France has iron ore and coal. Germany has coal, and the Netherlands has natural gas. Fast-flowing alpine rivers provide hydroelectric power. Even so, many countries have to import fuel. The beauty of the Alps is an important resource for tourism.

NORTHERN EUROPE

Northern Europe consists of two regions: the **British Isles** and **Scandinavia**. Iceland, to the west, is often considered part of Scandinavia. Fewer people live in the northern portion of the region, where rocky hills and low mountains make farming difficult. Farmland and plains stretch across the southern part of the region. Glaciers once covered Northern Europe, creating **fjords** along portions of the coastline and carving lakes in the interior.

Northern Europe's primary resources are its energy resources, forests and soils, and surrounding seas. Energy resources include oil

> **Circle the names of two important rivers in the region.**

> **Circle the energy resources of France. Underline the energy resources of Germany and the Netherlands.**

> **What two features were created by glaciers?**
> _____
> _____

> **Underline the energy resources of Northern Europe.**

and natural gas from North Sea deposits.
Hydroelectric energy is produced by the many
lakes and rivers. Iceland's hot springs produce
geothermal energy, or energy from the heat of
Earth's interior. Forests in Norway, Sweden, and
Finland provide timber. Fertile farmland in
southern portions of the region produce crops
such as wheat and potatoes. The seas and oceans
that surround the region have provided fish to the
people of Northern Europe for centuries.

Although much of the region is close to the
Arctic Circle, the climate is surprisingly mild
because of the North Atlantic Drift. Denmark,
the British Isles, and western Norway have a
marine west coast climate. Although they have
snow and frosts, the ports are not frozen for
much of the winter. Central Norway, Sweden,
and southern Finland have a humid continental
climate. Subarctic regions in northern
Scandinavia experience long, cold winters and
short summers. Iceland's tundra and ice cap
climates produce extremely cold temperatures
year round. Not surprisingly, most people in
Northern Europe live in urban areas and few live
in the far north.

> **Why is the climate mild in much of Northern Europe?**
> _____
> _____
> _____

CHALLENGE ACTIVITY

Critical Thinking: Evaluate How have landforms
and bodies of water affected activities in the
region? Give support for your answer.

DIRECTIONS Read each sentence and fill in the blank with the word in the word pair that best completes each sentence.

1. West-Central Europe's best farmland and largest cities are found on the _____. (**Northern European Plain/North Sea**)

2. The two most important rivers in West-Central Europe are the Rhine River and the _____. (**North Atlantic Drift/Danube River**)

3. West-Central Europe's _____ link the region's interior to the oceans. (**fjords/navigable rivers**)

4. Northern Europe is made up of the British Isles and _____. (**Scandinavia/Northern European Plain**)

5. Oil and natural gas deposits are found in the _____. (**North Sea/English Channel**)

6. Northern Europe experiences a mild climate due to the _____. (**geothermal energy/North Atlantic Drift**)

7. Energy produced from the heat of Earth's interior is called _____. (**geothermal energy/hydroelectric energy**)

British Isles	Danube River
English Channel	fjord
geothermal energy	navigable rivers
North Atlantic Drift	North Sea
Northern European Plain	Rhine River
Scandinavia	

DIRECTIONS Answer each question by writing a sentence that contains at least two words from the word bank.

8. Why are West-Central Europe's rivers important?

_____

_____

9. What are some of Northern Europe's energy resources?

_____

_____

Western Europe

MAIN IDEAS
1. During its history, France has been a kingdom, empire, colonial power, and republic.
2. The culture of France has contributed to the world's arts and ideas.
3. France today is a farming and manufacturing center.
4. The Benelux Countries have strong economies and high standards of living.

Key Terms and Places

Paris capital and largest city in France

Amsterdam capital of the Netherlands

The Hague seat of government in the Netherlands

Brussels capital of Belgium, headquarters of many international organizations

cosmopolitan characterized by many foreign influences

Lesson Summary
HISTORY OF FRANCE

In ancient times, Celtic people from eastern Europe settled in what is now France. Later, this land was conquered by the Romans and Franks. The Franks' ruler, Charlemagne, built a large empire and was crowned emperor of the Romans by the pope in 800. Later, the Normans claimed northwestern France. They became kings of England and ruled part of France until they were driven out by the French. During the 1500s to 1700s, France became a colonial power with colonies in Asia, Africa, and the Americas.

> Circle the names of three groups that ruled France during its early history.

In 1789 the French people overthrew their king in the French Revolution. Napoleon Bonaparte took power and conquered most of Europe, creating a vast empire. This ended in 1815 when European powers defeated his armies. During World Wars I and II, Germany invaded France. In the 1950s and 1960s, many French colonies declared independence. France is now a democratic republic.

> Underline the sentences that tell how Napoleon Bonaparte affected French history.

Guided Reading Workbook

THE CULTURE OF FRANCE

The French share a common heritage. Most speak French and are Catholic. Recently, France has become more diverse due to immigration. The French share a love of good food and company. The French have made major contributions to the arts and ideas—including impressionism, Gothic cathedrals, and Enlightenment ideas about government.

> Underline the sentences that describe the ways the French are alike.

FRANCE TODAY

France is Western Europe's largest country. **Paris** is a center of business, finance, learning, and culture. France has a strong economy and is the EU's top agricultural producer. Major crops include wheat and grapes, but tourism and the export of goods such as perfumes and wines are also vital to the economy.

THE BENELUX COUNTRIES

Belgium, the Netherlands, and Luxembourg are the Benelux Countries. Their location has led to invasions but has also promoted trade. All are densely populated, lie at low elevations between larger, stronger countries, and have strong economies and democratic governments. North Sea harbors have made the Netherlands a center for trade. Major cities include Rotterdam, **Amsterdam**, and **The Hague**. About 25 percent of the Netherlands lies below sea level. **Brussels**, Belgium, is a **cosmopolitan** city with many international organizations. The country is known for cheese, chocolate, cocoa, and lace. Luxembourg's economy is based on banking and steel and chemical production.

> Circle the names of the three Benelux Countries.

> Underline the sentence that tells how the Benelux Countries are alike.

Lesson 2, *continued*

CHALLENGE ACTIVITY

Critical Thinking: Draw Conclusions Write a
sentence that explains how the location of the
Benelux Countries has both helped and hurt
them.

DIRECTIONS Read each sentence and fill in the blank with the
word in the word pair that best completes the sentence.

1. Also known as the City of Lights, _____ is the capital of France.
   (Brussels/Paris)

2. The seat of government in the Netherlands is _____. **(Amsterdam/
   The Hague)**

3. Brussels, the capital of Belgium, is considered a _____ city because
   of its many foreign influences. **(cosmopolitan/sprawling)**

4. _____ is the capital of the Netherlands. **(Amsterdam/The Hague)**

DIRECTIONS Write a word or short phrase that has the same
meaning as the term given.

5. The Hague _____

6. Brussels _____

7. Benelux _____

Guided Reading Workbook

Western Europe

MAIN IDEAS
1. After a history of division and two world wars, Germany is now a unified country.
2. German culture, known for its contributions to music, literature, and science, is growing more diverse.
3. Germany today has Europe's largest economy, but eastern Germany faces challenges.
4. The Alpine Countries reflect German culture and have strong economies based on tourism and services.

Key Terms and Places

Berlin capital of Germany

Protestant those who protested against the Catholic Church

chancellor prime minister elected by Parliament who runs the government

Vienna Austria's capital and largest city

cantons districts of Switzerland's federal republic

neutral not taking sides in international conflict

Bern capital of Switzerland

Lesson Summary
HISTORY OF GERMANY

The land that is now Germany was a loose association of small states for hundreds of years. In 1871 Prussia united them to create Germany, which grew into a world power. After World War I, the German economy suffered and Adolf Hitler came to power. After its defeat in World War II, Germany was divided into democratic West Germany and Communist East Germany. **Berlin** was also divided. The Berlin Wall was built to stop East Germans from escaping to West Germany. In 1989 democracy movements swept Eastern Europe and communism collapsed. In 1990 East and West Germany were reunited.

> Why did Communist leaders build the Berlin Wall?
>
> _____
>
> _____
>
> _____

> What events helped East and West Germany reunite?
>
> _____
>
> _____
>
> _____
>
> _____

CULTURE OF GERMANY

Most people in Germany are ethnic Germans who speak German. Immigrants are making Germany more multicultural. Most people are either **Protestant** or Catholic. Germans have made important contributions to classical music, literature, chemistry, engineering, and medicine.

> **Most Germans belong to one or the other of which two religious groups?**
>
> _____
> _____

GERMANY TODAY

Germany is a leading European power. It is a federal republic governed by a parliament and a **chancellor**. It is Europe's largest economy, exporting many products, including cars. Germany's economy is based mainly on industries such as chemicals, engineering, and steel, but agriculture is also important. Acid rain from industry and vehicle exhaust has damaged trees and soil in Germany.

> **What economic activities have made Germany Europe's largest economy?**
>
> _____
> _____
> _____
> _____

THE ALPINE COUNTRIES

The Alpine Countries are Austria and Switzerland. They share much in common. Both were once part of the Holy Roman Empire, are landlocked, influenced by German culture, and prosperous. Austria was the center of the powerful Habsburg Empire that ruled much of Europe. Today, Austria is a modern, industrialized nation. **Vienna** is a center of music and fine arts. Austria has a strong economy with little unemployment. Service industries and tourism are important.

> **Underline the sentence that explains what the Alpine Countries have in common.**

Switzerland has been independent since the 1600s. It is a federal republic made up of 26 **cantons**. It is **neutral** and not a member of the EU or NATO. The Swiss speak several languages, including German and French. The capital, **Bern**, is centrally located. Switzerland is known for tourism and for its banks, watches, chocolate, and cheese.

> **List two important industries in the Alpine Countries.**
>
> _____
> _____

CHALLENGE ACTIVITY

Critical Thinking: Draw Inferences What are some factors that have contributed to the prosperity of the Alpine Countries?

DIRECTIONS Read each sentence and fill in the blank with the word in the word pair that best completes the sentence.

1. _____ is the capital of Germany. (**Vienna/Berlin**)

2. In Germany, a parliament elects a

   _____, or prime minister, who runs the government. (**canton/chancellor**)

3. Switzerland is made up of 26 districts called _____.

   (**cantons/chancellors**)

4. _____ is the capital of Austria and also its largest city.

   (**Berlin/Vienna**)

5. The capital of Switzerland, _____, is centrally located

   between the country's German- and French-speaking regions. (**Bern/Vienna**)

Berlin	Bern	cantons	chancellor
neutral	Protestant	Vienna	

DIRECTIONS Choose five terms from the word bank. Use these terms to write a summary of what you learned in this lesson.

_____

_____

_____

_____

_____

Western Europe

Lesson 4

> **MAIN IDEAS**
> 1. Invaders and a global empire have shaped the history of the British Isles.
> 2. British culture, such as government and music, has influenced much of the world.
> 3. Efforts to bring peace to Northern Ireland and maintain strong economies are important issues in the British Isles today.

Key Terms and Places

constitutional monarchy type of democracy in which a king or queen serves as head of state, but a legislature makes the laws

Magna Carta document that limited the powers of kings and required everyone to obey the law

disarm give up all weapons

London capital of the United Kingdom

Dublin capital of the Republic of Ireland

Lesson Summary
HISTORY

The Republic of Ireland and the United Kingdom make up the British Isles. The United Kingdom consists of England, Scotland, Wales, and Northern Ireland.

The Celts were early settlers of the British Isles. Later, Romans, Angles, Saxons, Vikings, and Normans invaded Britain. Over time, England grew in strength, and by the 1500s it had become a world power. England eventually formed the United Kingdom with Wales, Scotland, and Ireland. It developed a strong economy thanks to the Industrial Revolution and its colonies abroad.

The British Empire stretched around the world by 1900 but later declined. The Republic of Ireland won its independence, and by the mid-1900s Britain had given up most of its colonies.

> What two countries make up the British Isles?
>
> _____
>
> _____

> Underline the sentence that lists the countries that formed the United Kingdom.

CULTURE

The United Kingdom is a **constitutional monarchy**. England first limited the power of monarchs during the Middle Ages in a document called **Magna Carta**. This document influenced the governments of many countries. Ireland's president serves as head of state, but a prime minister and Parliament run the government.

The people of the British Isles share many cultural traits, but each region is also unique. The people of Ireland and Scotland keep many traditions alive, and immigrants from all over the world add new traits to the culture of the British Isles.

British popular culture has influenced people around the world. British literature and music are well known, and the English language is used in many countries.

> **In what ways are the governments of the United Kingdom and Ireland similar and different?**
>
> _____
> _____
> _____
> _____
> _____
> _____

> **Underline the sentence that describes how British popular culture has influenced other people.**

BRITISH ISLES TODAY

Efforts to maintain a powerful economy, the United Kingdom's relationship with the EU, and challenges to peace in Northern Ireland are key issues facing the British Isles today. In 2016 citizens of the UK voted to exit the EU, a departure nicknamed Brexit. In Northern Ireland, many Catholics feel they have not been treated fairly by Protestants. Some hope to unite with the Republic of Ireland. In the late 1990s peace talks led to the creation of a national assembly in Northern Ireland. However, some groups refused to **disarm**, delaying the peace process.

Maintaining powerful economies in the British Isles is a key issue today. **London** is a center for world trade, and the country has reserves of oil and natural gas in the North Sea. **Dublin** has attracted new industries like computers and electronics.

> **What three key issues face the British Isles today?**
>
> _____
> _____
> _____
> _____
> _____
> _____

CHALLENGE ACTIVITY

Critical Thinking: Identify Cause and Effect

Explain the factors that caused the development of a strong economy in the United Kingdom following its formation. Then explain two effects of the decline of the British Empire.

_____

_____

_____

_____

DIRECTIONS Read each sentence and fill in the blank with the word in the word pair that best completes the sentence.

1. Many Catholics in Northern Ireland hope to unite with

   _____. (**the Republic of Ireland/Wales**)

2. The capital of the United Kingdom is _____.
   (**London/Dublin**)

3. The nickname for the United Kingdom's departure from the EU is

   _____. (**Magna Carta/Brexit**)

4. A _____ is a government that has a monarch but a
   legislative body that makes the laws. (**Magna Carta/constitutional monarchy**)

DIRECTIONS Write three words or phrases that describe the term.

5. disarm _____

   _____

6. London _____

7. Dublin _____

   _____

8. Magna Carta _____

   _____

Western Europe

MAIN IDEAS
1. The history of Scandinavia dates back to the time of the Vikings.
2. Scandinavia today is known for its peaceful and prosperous countries.

Key Terms and Places

Vikings Scandinavian warriors who raided Europe in the early Middle Ages

Stockholm Sweden's capital and largest city

uninhabitable not able to support human settlement

Oslo the capital of Norway

Helsinki Finland's capital and largest city

geysers springs that shoot hot water and steam into the air

Lesson Summary
HISTORY

Vikings were Scandinavian warriors who raided Europe during the early Middle Ages. They were greatly feared and conquered the British Isles, Finland, and parts of France, Germany, and Russia.

Vikings were excellent sailors. They were the first Europeans to settle in Iceland and Greenland and the first Europeans to reach North America. They stopped raiding in the 1100s and focused on strengthening their kingdoms. Norway, Sweden, and Denmark competed for control of the region, and by the late 1300s Denmark ruled all the Scandinavian Kingdoms and territories. Sweden eventually broke away, taking Finland, and later Norway, with it. Norway, Finland, and Iceland became independent countries during the 1900s. Greenland remains part of Denmark as a self-ruling territory.

> Underline the sentence that explains the areas that Vikings explored.

> Which three countries did not become independent until the 1900s?
> _____
> _____
> _____

SCANDINAVIA TODAY

Scandinavians today have much in common, including similar political views, languages, and religions. They enjoy high standards of living, are well-educated, and get free health care. The countries have strong economies and large cities.

Sweden has the largest area and population. Most people live in large towns and cities in the south. **Stockholm** is Sweden's capital and largest city. Often called a floating city, it is built on 14 islands and part of the mainland. Although neutral, Sweden does play an active role in the UN and the EU.

Denmark is Scandinavia's smallest and most densely populated country. Its economy relies on farming and modern industries. Greenland is mostly covered with ice and **uninhabitable**. Most Greenlanders live on the southwest coast and rely heavily on Denmark for imports and economic aid.

Norway has one of the longest coastlines in the world. **Oslo** is Norway's capital, a leading seaport and industrial center. Oil and natural gas provide Norway with the highest per capita GDP in the region; however, oil fields in the North Sea are expected to run out during the next century. Norway's citizens have voted not to join the EU.

Finland relies on trade, and it exports paper and other forest products. Shipbuilding and electronics are also important. **Helsinki** is its capital and largest city.

Iceland has fertile farmland and rich fishing grounds. Tourists come to see its volcanoes, glaciers, and **geysers**. Geothermal energy heats many buildings.

Underline the sentence that lists traits Scandinavians have in common.

What is the largest country in area? What is the smallest? _____ _____

Why are tourists attracted to Iceland? _____ _____

CHALLENGE ACTIVITY

Critical Thinking: Make Inferences How do you think Norway might change if oil fields run out during the next century? Write a short paragraph to explain your answer.

Guided Reading Workbook

| geysers | Helsinki | Oslo |
| Stockholm | uninhabitable | Vikings |

DIRECTIONS Answer each question by writing a sentence that contains at least one word from the word bank.

1. How were longships used by Scandinavian warriors?

   _____

2. Why do most people in Greenland live on the southwest coast?

   _____

   _____

3. What is Norway's capital like?

   _____

4. How are many homes in Iceland heated?

   _____

5. What city in Scandinavia is often called a floating city and why?

   _____

Lesson 1

MAIN IDEAS
1. The physical features of Eastern Europe include wide open plains, rugged mountain ranges, and many rivers.
2. The climate and vegetation of Eastern Europe differ widely in the north and the south.

Key Terms and Places

Carpathians low mountain range stretching from the Alps to the Black Sea area

Balkan Peninsula one of the largest peninsulas in Europe; extends into the Mediterranean

Chernobyl nuclear power plant in Ukraine

Lesson Summary
PHYSICAL FEATURES

The landforms of Eastern Europe stretch across the region in broad bands of plains and mountains. The Northern European Plain covers most of Northern Europe. South of this plain is a low mountain range called the **Carpathians**. It extends from the Alps to the Black Sea area. South and west of the Carpathians is another large plain, the Great Hungarian Plain, located mostly in Hungary. South of this plain are the Dinaric Alps and Balkan Mountains. These mountain ranges cover most of the **Balkan Peninsula**, one of Europe's largest peninsulas. It extends into the Mediterranean Sea.

Eastern Europe has many water bodies that are important routes for transportation and trade. The Adriatic Sea lies to the southwest. The Black Sea is east of the region. The Baltic Sea is in the far north. Some parts of the Baltic freeze over in winter, reducing its usefulness.

The rivers that flow through Eastern Europe are also important for trade and transportation,

> Circle three mountain ranges in Eastern Europe.

> List two reasons that rivers are important to the economy of Eastern Europe.
>
> _____
>
> _____

especially the Danube River. The Danube begins in Germany and crosses nine countries before it empties into the Black Sea. This river is very important to Eastern Europe's economy. Some of the region's largest cities are along its banks. Dams on the river provide electricity for the region. This river has become very polluted from heavy use.

> **Why is the Danube so polluted?**
> _____

CLIMATE AND VEGETATION

Types of climates and vegetation in Eastern Europe vary widely. The shores of the Baltic Sea in the far north have the coldest climate, with long, harsh winters. The area does not get much rain but is often foggy. Its cold, damp climate allows huge forests to grow.

> **Underline the descriptions of climate found in the Baltic region.**

The interior plains have a much milder climate than the Baltic region. Winters can be very cold, but summers are mild. The western parts of the interior plains get more rain than the eastern parts. Because of its varied climate, there are many types of vegetation. Forests cover much of the north, and grassy plains lie in the south.

In 1986 Eastern Europe's forests were damaged by a major nuclear accident at **Chernobyl** in Ukraine. An explosion released huge amounts of radiation into the air that poisoned forests and ruined soil across the region.

The Balkan coast along the Adriatic Sea has a Mediterranean climate, with warm summers and mild winters. Its beaches attract tourists. The area does not get much rain, so there are not many forests. The land is covered by shrubs and trees that do not need much water.

> **Why is the vegetation along the Balkan coast different from the vegetation of the Baltic region?**
> _____
> _____
> _____
> _____
> _____
> _____

CHALLENGE ACTIVITY

Critical Thinking: Analyze Information How has climate affected the vegetation in Eastern Europe? Explain your answer in a brief paragraph.

Adriatic Sea	Balkan Mountains	Balkan Peninsula	Carpathians
Chernobyl	Danube River	function	radiation

DIRECTIONS On the line provided before each statement, write **T** if a statement is true and **F** if a statement is false. If the statement is false, write the correct term from the word bank on the line after each sentence that makes the sentence a true statement.

_____ 1. The <u>Balkan Mountains</u> are a low mountain range that stretch in a long arc from the Alps to the Black Sea area.

_____

_____ 2. The Black Sea serves the same function as the <u>Carpathians</u>; they are both important trade routes.

_____

_____ 3. A nuclear explosion at the <u>Chernobyl</u> power plant released huge amounts of radiation into the air.

_____

_____ 4. The <u>Danube River</u> begins in Germany and flows through nine countries before emptying into the Black Sea.

_____

_____ 5. One of the largest landforms in Europe, the <u>Chernobyl</u> extends south into the Mediterranean Sea.

_____

Eastern Europe

Lesson 2

MAIN IDEAS
1. History ties Poland and the Baltic Republics together.
2. The cultures of Poland and the Baltic Republics differ in language and religion but share common customs.
3. Economic growth is a major issue in the region today.

Key Terms and Places

infrastructure set of resources—like roads, airports, and factories—that a country needs in order to support economic activities

Warsaw capital of Poland

Lesson Summary

HISTORY

The groups who settled around the Baltic Sea in ancient times developed into the Estonians, Latvians, Lithuanians, and Polish. Each group had its own language and culture, but in time they became connected by a shared history. By the Middle Ages, each had formed an independent kingdom. Lithuania and Poland were the largest and strongest. They ruled large parts of Eastern and Northern Europe. Latvia and Estonia were smaller, weaker, and often invaded.

In the 1900s two world wars greatly damaged the Baltic region. In World War I, millions died in Poland, and thousands more were killed in the Baltic countries. The region also suffered greatly during World War II. This war began when Germany invaded Poland. Millions more died. While fighting the Germans, troops from the Soviet Union invaded Poland and occupied Estonia, Latvia, and Lithuania.

After World War II ended, the Soviet Union took over much of Eastern Europe, making Estonia, Latvia, and Lithuania part of the Soviet Union. The Soviets also forced Poland to accept a Communist government. In 1989 Poland

> How did the Baltic Republics lose their independence after World War II?
>
> _____
> _____
> _____
> _____
> _____
> _____

Guided Reading Workbook

rejected communism and elected new leaders. In 1991 the Baltic Republics broke away from the Soviet Union. They became independent countries again.

> Underline the sentences that tell how the governments of the Baltic countries changed beginning in 1989.

CULTURE

The Baltic countries differ from each other in languages and religion but are alike in other ways. Latvian and Lithuanian languages are similar, but Estonian is like Finnish, the language spoken in Finland. Polish is more like languages of countries farther south. Most Polish people and Lithuanians are Roman Catholics because they traded with Catholic countries. Latvians and Estonians are Lutherans because these countries were once ruled by Sweden, where most people are Lutherans.

These countries' people share many customs and practices. They eat similar foods and practice crafts such as ceramics, painting, and embroidery, a type of decorative sewing. They also enjoy music and dance.

> What economic problems did Soviet rule cause for Poland and the Baltic Republics?
> _____
> _____
> _____
> _____
> _____
> _____

THE REGION TODAY

The economies of Baltic countries suffered because of the long Soviet rule. The Soviets did not build a decent **infrastructure** to support the economy, so the Baltic countries could not produce as many goods as Western countries. Poland and the Baltic Republics are working hard to rebuild their economies. As a result, cities like **Warsaw**, Poland's capital, have become major industrial centers. To help their economies grow, many Baltic countries are trying to attract more tourism. Since the Soviet Union collapsed in 1991, cities like Warsaw and Krakow have attracted tourists with their rich culture, historic sites, and cool summer climates.

> What new source of income have the Baltic countries found?
> _____

CHALLENGE ACTIVITY

Critical Thinking: Understand Effects Imagine that you are a newly elected leader of a Baltic country. Write a speech that tells what you will do to improve the country's economy.

DIRECTIONS Read each sentence and fill in the blank with the word in the word pair that best completes the sentence.

1. The Soviets failed to build a strong

   _____, which has weakened

   the economies of the Baltic countries.

   (embroidery/infrastructure)

2. By the Middle Ages, the kingdoms of Lithuania

   and _____ were large and

   strong. **(Poland/Warsaw)**

3. _____ is the capital of Poland. **(Warsaw/Krakow)**

4. The _____ include(s) Latvia, Estonia, and Lithuania.

   (infrastructure/Baltic Republics)

5. _____ is a type of decorative sewing that is popular

   among people in the Baltic region. **(Krakow/Embroidery)**

Baltic Republics	embroidery	infrastructure
Krakow	Poland	Warsaw

DIRECTIONS Choose four of the terms from the word bank. On a separate sheet of paper, use these words to write a short story that relates to the lesson.

_____

_____

Eastern Europe

Lesson 3

> **MAIN IDEAS**
> 1. The histories and cultures of inland Eastern Europe vary from country to country.
> 2. Most of inland Eastern Europe today has stable governments, strong economies, and influential cities.

Key Terms and Places

Prague capital of the Czech Republic

Kiev present-day city where the Rus built a settlement

Commonwealth of Independent States CIS, an international alliance that meets to discuss issues such as trade and immigration that affect former Soviet republics

Budapest capital of Hungary

Lesson Summary
HISTORY AND CULTURE

Inland Eastern Europe consists of the Czech Republic, Slovakia, Hungary, Ukraine, Belarus, and Moldova. The region is located on the Northern European and Hungarian plains. The area of the Czech Republic and Slovakia was settled by Slavs, people from Asia who moved into Europe by AD 1000. In time, more powerful countries like Austria conquered these Slavic kingdoms. After World War I, land was taken away from Austria to create the nation of Czechoslovakia. In 1993 Czechoslovakia split into the Czech Republic and Slovakia.

The Czech Republic and Slovakia are located near Western Europe, with which they have much in common. Many people are Roman Catholic. The architecture of **Prague** shows Western influences.

In the 900s Magyar people invaded what is now Hungary. The Magyars influenced Hungarian culture, especially the Hungarian

> What group of people settled the area of the Czech Republic and Slovakia?
> _____

> Circle the country that land was taken away from to create Czechoslovakia.

language. In fact, people in Hungary today still refer to themselves as Magyars.

Ukraine, Belarus, and Moldova were also settled by Slavs, who were then conquered by Vikings. In the 800s a group called the Rus built the settlement that is now **Kiev** in Ukraine. The rulers of Kiev created a huge empire that became part of Russia in the late 1700s. In 1922 Russia became the Soviet Union. Ukraine, Belarus, and Moldova became Soviet republics. After the breakup of the Soviet Union in 1991, these countries became independent. Russia has strongly influenced their cultures. Most people are Orthodox Christians, and the Ukrainian and Belarusian languages are written in the Cyrillic, or Russian, alphabet.

> Underline two ways the cultures of Ukraine, Belarus, and Moldova have been influenced by Russia.

INLAND EASTERN EUROPE TODAY

All inland Eastern European countries were once either part of the Soviet Union or run by Soviet-influenced Communist governments. People had few freedoms. The Soviets did a poor job of managing these economies. Since the collapse of the Soviet Union, Hungary, Slovakia, the Czech Republic, Ukraine, and Moldova have become republics. The people elect their leaders. Belarus also claims to be a republic, but it is really a dictatorship.

> How have the governments of the region changed since the collapse of the Soviet Union?
>
> _____
>
> _____

The people of Ukraine are divided about whether to have a closer connection to Western democracies or Russia. The eastern part has more in common with Russia, while western Ukraine is similar to Europe. In 2014 Russia took over the eastern part of Ukraine known as Crimea. Many governments do not accept Russia's claim to the area.

Countries of Eastern Europe belong to
international organizations. Belarus, Ukraine,
and Moldova belong to the **Commonwealth of
Independent States**. Its members meet to talk
about issues like trade and immigration. The
Czech Republic, Slovakia, Romania, Bulgaria,
and Hungary seek closer ties to the West and
belong to the EU. Slovakia, Hungary, and
Ukraine have become prosperous industrial
centers.

> Why have some Eastern
> European countries joined
> the EU?
>
> _____
> _____

The capital cities of the region are also
economic and cultural centers. Prague, Kiev, and
Budapest are especially important. They are the
most prosperous cities in the region, home to
important leaders, universities, and cultural sites.
Tourists from around the world visit these cities.

CHALLENGE ACTIVITY

Critical Thinking: Evaluate Write a paragraph
that explains how the location of inland Eastern
Europe has affected its culture and history.

| Budapest | Commonwealth of Independent States | Kiev |
| Magyars | Prague | Slavs |

DIRECTIONS Read each sentence and choose the correct term from the word bank to replace the underlined phrase. Write the term in the space provided and then define the term in your own words.

1. Belarus, Ukraine, and Moldova are members of <u>this organization</u>. _____

   _____

   Your definition: _____

   _____

2. <u>This group of fierce invaders</u> swept into Hungary and influenced the language there. _____

   Your definition: _____

3. <u>This</u> is the most prosperous and cultural city in the Czech Republic.

   _____

   Your definition: _____

4. The Rus established <u>this city</u> in the 800s, which still stands in Ukraine today.

   _____

   Your definition: _____

   _____

5. The Czech Republic and Slovakia were settled by <u>this group of people</u>.

   _____

   Your definition: _____

Guided Reading Workbook

MAIN IDEAS
1. The history of the Balkan countries is one of conquest and conflict.
2. The cultures of the Balkan countries are shaped by the many ethnic groups who live there.
3. Civil wars and weak economies are major challenges to the region today.

Key Terms and Places

ethnocentrism belief that one's own culture or ethnic group is superior

ethnic cleansing effort to remove all members of a group from a country or region

Lesson Summary
HISTORY

The Balkan Peninsula has been ruled by many different groups. In ancient times, the Greeks founded colonies near the Black Sea. This area is now Bulgaria and Romania. Next, the Romans conquered most of the area between the Adriatic Sea and the Danube River. When the Roman Empire divided into west and east in the AD 300s, the Balkan Peninsula became part of the Byzantine Empire. Under Byzantine rule, many people became Orthodox Christians.

Over 1,000 years later, Muslim Ottoman Turks conquered the Byzantine Empire. Many people in the Balkans became Muslims. Ottoman rule lasted until the 1800s, when the people of the Balkans drove the Ottomans out. They then created their own kingdoms.

In the late 1800s the Austria-Hungarian Empire took over part of the peninsula. To protest the takeover, a man from Serbia shot the heir to the Austro-Hungarian throne. This event led to World War I. After the war, Europe's leaders combined many formerly independent countries into Yugoslavia. In the 1990s this

> Underline the names of groups or empires that ruled the Balkan Peninsula until the 1800s.

> Underline the sentences that explain the events that led to World War I.

country broke apart. Ethnic and religious conflict led to its collapse.

CULTURE

The Balkans are Europe's most diverse region. People practice different religions and speak many different languages. Most people are Christians. They are either Orthodox, Roman Catholic, or Protestant. Islam is also practiced. Albania is the only country in Europe that is mostly Muslim. Most people speak Slavic languages that are related to Russian. People in Romania speak a language that comes from Latin. Albanian is like no other language in the world, as is the language spoken by the Roma people.

> **What makes the Balkans Europe's most diverse region?**
> _____
> _____
> _____
> _____

THE BALKANS TODAY

Balkan countries were once run by Communist governments. Poor economic planning has hurt the economies of the region. It is still the poorest region in Europe today.

There are also serious problems between the different religious and ethnic groups. When Yugoslavia broke apart, the new countries that formed had violent conflicts. **Ethnocentrism**—the belief that one's own culture or ethnic group is superior—led to **ethnic cleansing**. Religious or ethnic groups used threats and violence against people from other cultures who would not leave. In 1995 troops from all over the world came to Bosnia and Herzegovina to help end the fighting.

Since 2008, ten countries share the Balkan Peninsula. Macedonia and Slovenia were the first to break away from Yugoslavia. When Croatia broke away, fighting started between ethnic Croats and Serbs. Peace did not return until many Serbs left Croatia. Bosnia and Herzegovina also had terrible ethnic fighting. Serbia, the largest country to emerge from the former

> **What caused the violence in the Balkans after Yugoslavia broke apart?**
> _____
> _____
> _____

> **What ended the fighting in Bosnia and Herzegovina?**
> _____
> _____
> _____

Yugoslavia, also saw terrible fighting. Both
Montenegro and Kosovo separated from Serbia.

The Balkans includes three other countries.
Albania and Romania are poor and have serious
economic and political problems. Bulgaria has a
strong economy based on industry and tourism.

CHALLENGE ACTIVITY

Critical Thinking: Predict Write a paragraph that
explains how ethnic diversity could be an
advantage for the Balkan countries in the future.

DIRECTIONS Look at each set of terms following each number. On
the line provided, write the letter of the term that does not relate to
the others.

_____ 1. a. Protestant   b. Orthodox   c. Catholic   d. Slavic

_____ 2. a. World War I   b. Serbia   c. Germanic   d. Austro-Hungarians

_____ 3. a. Albania   b. Hungary   c. Croatia   d. Slovenia

_____ 4. a. Macedonia   b. Yugoslavia   c. violence   d. ethnic cleansing

_____ 5. a. Balkans   b. Greeks   c. Romans   d. Ottomans

Albania	Balkans	ethnic cleansing
ethnocentrism	Hungary	Orthodox
Slavic	Soviet Union	Yugoslavia

DIRECTIONS Choose at least three of the terms from the word bank. On a separate sheet of paper, use these words to write a summary of what you learned in the lesson.

Russia and the Caucasus

Lesson 1

MAIN IDEAS
1. The physical features of Russia and the Caucasus include plains, mountains, and rivers.
2. Russia's cold climate contrasts sharply with the warmer Caucasus.
3. Russia has a wealth of natural resources, but many are hard to access.

Key Terms and Places

Ural Mountains mountain range where Europe and Asia meet

Caspian Sea world's largest inland sea; borders the Caucasus Mountains

Caucasus Mountains mountain range that covers much of the area between the Black Sea and the Caspian Sea

Moscow capital of Russia

Siberia vast region in Russia stretching from the Urals to the Pacific Ocean

Volga River longest river in Europe, located in western Russia

taiga forest of mainly evergreen trees covering much of Russia

Lesson Summary
PHYSICAL FEATURES

The continents of Asia and Europe meet in Russia's **Ural Mountains**. Together, Asia and Europe form the large landmass of Eurasia. A large part of Eurasia is Russia, the world's largest country.

The Caucasus is the area south of Russia between the Black Sea and the **Caspian Sea**. It is named for the **Caucasus Mountains**, and includes Georgia, Armenia, Azerbaijan, and parts of southern Russia. The area is mostly rugged upland.

Russia's landforms vary from west to east. The fertile Northern European Plain, Russia's heartland, extends across western Russia. Most Russians live in this area, and **Moscow**, Russia's capital, is located there. Going east, the plain rises to form the low Ural Mountains. The area between the Urals and the Pacific Ocean is **Siberia**.

Which two continents meet in the Ural Mountains?
_____
_____

Circle the names of the three countries that are found in the Caucasus.

What is the capital of Russia?
_____

Lesson 1, *continued*

The West Siberian Plain is a huge, flat, marshy area. It is one of the largest plains in the world. The rivers in this plain flow toward the Arctic Ocean. East of this plain is an upland called the Central Siberian Plateau. High mountain ranges run through southern and eastern Siberia.

Eastern Siberia is called the Russian Far East, which includes the Kamchatka Peninsula and several islands. This area is part of the Ring of Fire, known for its volcanoes and earthquakes. There are over 120 volcanoes, 20 of which are still active. South of the peninsula lie the Sakhalin islands seized from Japan after World War II. Japan still claims ownership of the Kuril islands.

> **What is the Ring of Fire?**
> _____
> _____
> _____

Some of the longest rivers in the world flow through the region. The **Volga River** is the longest river in Europe and the core of Russia's river network. It runs south to the Caspian Sea and is linked to the Don River and Baltic Sea by canals. Other rivers include the Ob, Yenisey, and Lena rivers, which flow northward to the Arctic Ocean. Many of Russia's rivers stay frozen for much of the year, which can slow shipping and trade.

> **What is the longest river in Europe?**
> _____

Russia also has some 200,000 lakes. Lake Baikal is the world's deepest lake. It is called the Jewel of Siberia, but logging and factories have polluted the water. Russians are trying to clean it.

In the Caucasus, lowlands lie between the Black Sea, the region's western border, and the Caspian Sea, the eastern border. The Black Sea is an important trade route because it links to the Mediterranean. The Caspian Sea is a saltwater lake—the largest inland sea in the world.

CLIMATE AND PLANT LIFE

Russia is cold because it lies far north, partly in the Arctic Circle. It has short summers and long, snowy winters. Most Russians live west of the

> **Underline the sentence that explains why Russia is so cold.**

Urals, where the climate is milder than the north and east.

Russia's northern coast is tundra, and most of the ground is permafrost, or permanently frozen soil. Only small plants like mosses grow. Areas closer to the Atlantic Ocean have more moisture than inland regions. South of the tundra is the vast **taiga**, a forest of mainly evergreen trees that covers half of Russia.

In the Caucasus, moist air from the Mediterranean Sea provides a warm and wet subtropical climate zone along the Black Sea. Tourists used to go to this area until ethnic conflict made it dangerous to travel there. It is cooler in the uplands. Azerbaijan is hot and dry. The Caucasus is one of the most biologically diverse regions on Earth. The climate and soil are good for farming, and the mountains are home to impressive forests and wildflowers.

> **What causes the subtropical climate in parts of the Caucasus?**
> _____
> _____

NATURAL RESOURCES

Russia has a wealth of natural resources, including timber, metals, precious gems, and rich soils for farming. Energy resources, such as oil, natural gas, and coal, are among its largest exports. These resources have been poorly managed, however. Many resources near populated areas are gone, and it is hard to reach resources in more remote areas like Siberia.

> **What energy resources are important exports for Russia?**
> _____
> _____
> _____

CHALLENGE ACTIVITY

Critical Thinking: Make Generalizations Based on what you have read so far, write a short paragraph about what it might be like to live in Russia.

DIRECTIONS Read each sentence and fill in the blank with the word in the word pair that best completes the sentence.

1. It is in the _____ that the continents of Europe and Asia meet. (**Caucasus Mountains/Ural Mountains**)

2. The _____ provides an important transportation route through Russia. (**Black Sea/Volga River**)

3. The _____ links the Caucasus to the Mediterranean. (**Caspian Sea/Black Sea**)

4. The Ring of Fire is located in eastern _____. (**Siberia/Moscow**)

5. The vast forest of evergreen trees that covers about half of Russia is called the _____. (**tundra/taiga**)

Black Sea	Caspian Sea	Caucasus Mountains
Moscow	Siberia	taiga
tundra	Ural Mountains	Volga River

DIRECTIONS Choose four of the terms from the word bank. On a separate sheet of paper, use these words to write a story or poem that relates to the lesson.

Russia and the Caucasus

Lesson 2

MAIN IDEAS

1. The Russian Empire grew under powerful leaders, but unrest and war led to its end.
2. The Soviet Union emerged as a Communist superpower with rigid government control.
3. Russia's history and diversity have influenced its culture.
4. The Russian Federation is working to develop democracy and a market economy.
5. Russia's physical geography, cities, and economy define its many culture regions.
6. Russia faces a number of serious challenges.

Key Terms and Places

Kiev early center of Russia, now the capital of Ukraine

Cyrillic form of the Greek alphabet

czar emperor

Bolsheviks Communist group that seized power during the Russian Revolution

gulags Soviet labor camps

dachas Russian country houses

St. Petersburg city founded by Peter the Great and styled after those of Western Europe

smelters factories that produce metal ores

Trans-Siberian Railway longest single rail line in the world, running from Moscow to Vladivostok on the east coast

Chechnya Russian republic in the Caucasus Mountains, an area of ethnic conflict

Lesson Summary
THE RUSSIAN EMPIRE

The Slavs came from Asia and settled in the area of what is now Ukraine and western Russia. In the AD 800s, Viking traders from Scandinavia, called Rus, invaded the Slavs. They created the first Russian state of Kievan, which centered around the city of **Kiev**. Kiev is now the capital of Ukraine.

Over time, missionaries introduced Orthodox Christianity and **Cyrillic**, a form of the Greek alphabet that Russians still use today. This alphabet is one of the differences between Russian and European languages, which developed from Latin.

In the 1200s Mongol invaders called Tatars conquered Kiev. Local Russian princes ruled several states under the Mongols. Muscovy became the strongest state, with Moscow its main city. After about 200 years, Muscovy's prince Ivan III seized control from the Mongols. Then in the 1540s, his grandson Ivan IV crowned himself **czar**, or emperor. He had total power and became known as Ivan the Terrible because he was a cruel and savage ruler.

Muscovy developed into the country of Russia. Peter the Great and then Catherine the Great ruled as czars, building Russia into a huge empire and world power. Under their rule, east-to-west trade along the Silk Road increased. Spices, teas, cotton, silk, and more came from as far away as India and the Ottoman Empire. These trade routes also spread disease.

By the nineteenth century, a north–south "Cotton Road" brought cotton to Russia from India, Egypt, South Asia, and the United States. Russian industrialists used it to create thriving textile mills during the Industrial Revolution. Yet, Russia remained mostly a country of poor farmers, while the czars and nobles had most of the wealth.

In the early 1900s the Russian people began demanding improvements. Unrest, World War I, and other problems weakened the Russian empire. In 1917 the czar lost support and was forced to give up the throne. The **Bolsheviks**, a Russian Communist group, seized power in the Russian Revolution. They killed the czar and his family. Bolshevik leaders formed the Union

What is Cyrillic?
_____
_____
_____

Circle the names of two czars who built Russia into a world power.

Underline the sentence that explains why the Russian people began demanding improvements.

Who were the Bolsheviks?
_____
_____
_____

of Soviet Socialist Republics (USSR), or the
Soviet Union, in 1922.

THE SOVIET UNION

The Soviet Union became a Communist country,
led by Vladimir Lenin. After Lenin's death in
1924, Joseph Stalin ruled as a brutal dictator. He
set up a command economy, where the
government owns all businesses and farms and
makes all economic decisions. It strictly
controlled its people. Anyone who spoke out
against the government was jailed, exiled, or
killed. Millions of people were sent to **gulags**,
harsh Soviet labor camps often located in Siberia.

> **What is a command economy?**
> _____
> _____
> _____
> _____

During World War II, the Soviet Union sided
with the Allies. Millions of Soviet citizens died.
After the war, Stalin built a protective buffer
around the Soviet Union to prevent invasion. He
did this by setting up Communist governments in
Eastern Europe. The United States saw this as a
threat. This created the Cold War, a period of
tense rivalry between the two countries, where
they competed to develop powerful weapons.

> **What did Stalin do to create a protective buffer around the Soviet Union?**
> _____
> _____

The Soviet Union grew weak in the 1980s, in
part because of its economy. Under its leader,
Mikhail Gorbachev, the country began to loosen
government control. The Soviet republics began
to push for independence, leading to the collapse
of the Soviet Union in 1991. It broke into 15
independent countries, including Russia.

RUSSIA'S CULTURE TODAY

More than 140 million people live in Russia.
Most are ethnic Russians, or Slavs, but Russia
also has many other ethnic groups. The Soviet
government had opposed religion and it
controlled culture. Today, the main faith is
Russian Orthodox Christian, but other religions
are practiced. The country celebrates a variety of
traditional holidays. Russia has made many

> **How many people live in Russia today?**
> _____

contributions to the arts and sciences, especially
in ballet and space research.

THE RUSSIAN FEDERATION TODAY

When the Soviet Union broke apart, Russia had
to create a new government. The Russian
Federation is a federal republic, which divides
power between national and local governments.
Voters elect a president, who then appoints a
prime minister. The Federal Assembly makes the
country's laws. It is similar to the parliamentary
system of the UK.

> Underline the sentence that explains how the Russian Federation divides power.

Russians have more freedom today as the
country moves toward democracy. However,
there are still problems of government corruption
that have slowed progress. The country is also
moving to a market economy based on free trade
and competition. Many businesses and farms are
now privately owned. Russia produces and
exports oil, natural gas, timber, metals, chemicals,
and crops like grains. Heavy, light, and service
industries are all important parts of the economy.

> What is a market economy?
>
> _____
>
> _____
>
> _____

About 75 percent of Russians live in cities,
where there is a large range of consumer goods,
restaurants, and stores. Some Russians have
become very wealthy and own **dachas** in the
country, but the average person still has a low
standard of living.

CULTURE REGIONS

Four western culture regions—Moscow, St.
Petersburg, Volga River, and Ural Mountains
areas—make up Russia's heartland. These
regions are home to the vast majority of Russia's
people.

> Circle the four western culture regions of Russia.

Moscow is Russia's capital and largest city. The
Kremlin holds Russia's government offices, as
well as beautiful palaces and gold-domed
churches. Moscow is a huge industrial region.

St. Petersburg was founded by Peter the Great and styled after cities of Western Europe. It was Russia's capital for some 200 years. Its location on the Gulf of Finland has made the city an important trade center.

The Volga River of the Volga region is a major shipping route and source of hydroelectric power. Factories here process oil and gas. The Caspian Sea provides black caviar.

The Urals region is an important mining area. Factories called **smelters** process metal ores, copper, and iron.

Siberia, another of Russia's culture regions, is east of the Urals. Winters there are long and severe. Siberia has many natural resources, but accessing them is difficult. Lumber, mining, and oil production are the most important industries. There are few towns in this region, and most follow the route of the **Trans-Siberian Railway**, the longest single rail line in the world.

Siberia's coastal areas and islands along the Pacific Ocean are known as the Russian Far East. This culture region's resources include timber, rich soils, oil, minerals, and fishing. Vladivostock is the region's main seaport.

Where is St. Petersburg located?
_____

What is notable about the Trans-Siberian Railway?
_____
_____

RUSSIA'S CHALLENGES

Since 1991 Russia has made great progress, but the change to a market economy has caused prices and unemployment to rise. Also, the gap between rich and poor has widened. Other problems are a falling population and serious pollution, which has harmed Russia's environment. The country has not protected its natural resources, causing further damage to the environment.

There is also ongoing tension between Russia and its neighbors. In 2013 Russia took over the part of Ukraine called Crimea. Ukraine considers this a violation of international law.

Circle two problems that are causing harm to Russia's environment.

Guided Reading Workbook

Russia also faces ethnic conflicts with the
Russian republic of **Chechnya**, a Muslim area.
Some people want independence, and this has led
to fighting and terrorism in the region.

CHALLENGE ACTIVITY

Critical Thinking: Draw Inferences Based on what
you have learned about each region, which area
do you think holds the most potential
economically for Russia? Why?

DIRECTIONS Look at each set of four terms. On the line provided,
write the letter of the term that does not relate to the others.

_____ 1. a. market economy   b. Stalin   c. Siberia   d. gulags

_____ 2. a. Cold War   b. weapons   c. Bolsheviks   d. arms race

_____ 3. a. communism   b. Cold War   c. Soviet Union   d. czar

_____ 4. a. Vikings   b. Siberia   c. Kiev   d. Rus

_____ 5. a. St. Petersburg   b. Moscow   c. Volga River   d. Chechnya

Bolsheviks	Chechnya	Cold War
communism	czar	gulags
market economy	Siberia	St. Petersburg

DIRECTIONS Choose five of the terms from the word bank. On a
separate sheet of paper, use these words to write a summary of what
you learned in the lesson.

Russia and the Caucasus

Lesson 3

MAIN IDEAS
1. Many groups have ruled and influenced the Caucasus during its long history.
2. Today, the Caucasus republics are working to improve their economies but struggle with ethnic unrest and conflict.

Key Terms and Places

Tbilisi capital of Georgia

Yerevan capital of Armenia

Baku capital of Azerbaijan, center of a large oil-refining industry

Lesson Summary

HISTORY

The Caucasus lies in the Caucasus Mountains between the Black Sea and the Caspian Sea, where Europe blends with Asia. The region reflects a range of cultural influences and at one time or another has been ruled or invaded by Persians, Greeks, Romans, Arabs, Turks, Mongols, and Russians.

In the early 1800s Russia took over much of the Caucasus, but the Ottoman Turks held western Armenia. Before and during World War I, Armenians were targets of ethnic cleansing by the Turks. Hundreds of thousands were removed by force or killed. After the war, Armenia, Azerbaijan, and Georgia gained independence, but by the early 1920s they became part of the Soviet Union. They regained independence when the Soviet Union fell in 1991.

> **Which groups have ruled or invaded the Caucasus?**
> _____
> _____
> _____

> **What happened to the Caucasus countries in the early 1920s?**
> _____
> _____

THE CAUCASUS TODAY

Although the region has a long history, the Caucasus countries have had to create new governments and economies. Progress has been slowed by ethnic unrest and conflicts. The countries have similar governments. An elected president governs each nation, and an appointed

> **Circle the reasons for the slow progress of the Caucasus countries.**

Guided Reading Workbook

prime minister runs each government. An elected parliament, or legislature, makes the laws.

Georgia is located in the Caucasus Mountains, east of the Black Sea. **Tbilisi** is the capital. About 70 percent of the people are ethnic Georgians and belong to the Georgian Orthodox Church. Georgian is the official language, with its own alphabet, but many other languages are spoken.

Georgia has struggled with unrest and civil war since independence. Georgians peacefully forced out their president in 2003. However, ethnic groups in northern Georgia continue to fight for independence from the rest of the country. Georgia's unrest has hurt its economy, but it is helped by international aid. The country's economy is based on services and farming. Other industries include steel, mining, wine, and tourism in Black Sea resorts.

> **Why is there unrest in northern Georgia?**
> _____
> _____
> _____

Armenia is a small, landlocked country south of Georgia. **Yerevan** is the capital. Most of the people are Armenian and belong to the Armenian Orthodox Church.

Armenia fought a war with Azerbaijan in the early 1990s. Armenia took over an area of Azerbaijan where most people were ethnic Armenian. Although there was a cease-fire in 1994, the area is still controlled by Armenian forces. The conflict remains unsettled and has hurt Armenia's economy, but international aid is helping. Diamond processing is now a growing industry.

> **Underline the sentence that explains why Armenia and Azerbaijan got into a war.**

Azerbaijan is east of Armenia and borders the Caspian Sea. The Azeri make up 90 percent of the population, and the country is mostly Muslim. Oil, found along the Caspian Sea, is the most important part of the economy. **Baku**, the capital, is the center of this industry, which has led to strong economic growth. Problems include corruption, poverty, and refugees as a result of the conflict with Armenia.

> **What is the most important part of Azerbaijan's economy?**
> _____

Lesson 3, *continued*

CHALLENGE ACTIVITY

Critical Thinking: Compare and Contrast Describe
the similarities and differences between the
Caucasus countries.

DIRECTIONS Write three words or phrases that describe each term.

1. Caspian Sea _____

2. Baku _____

DIRECTIONS Read each sentence and fill in the blank with the
word in the word pair that best completes the sentence.

3. The capital of Armenia is _____. (**Baku/Yerevan**)

4. _____ is the capital of Georgia. (**Yerevan/Tbilisi**)

5. Oil is the most important part of _____'s economy.
   (**Tbilisi/Azerbaijan**)

6. Georgia, Armenia, and Azerbaijan all lie south of the _____.
   (**Black Sea/Caucasus Mountains**)

7. The Armenians were targets of _____.
   (**ethnic cleansing/Yerevan**)